To, Greg and Judy
wealth be with you always!
You'll will always be enlighted by great people

Escape to Riches

God Bless!

The Life of Phillip Boon Lim

[signature] 8/19/17

Martha Rose Woodward

Phillip Lim

Author's Note: Phillip Lim is a natural born storyteller. I decided early on that his story needed to be told in his own words. For most of this project, we turned on a tape recorder and Phillip spoke. My part was to type his words and join the story together in a timeline and to match up his life to the history of the times. Phillip's way of using English is endearing. He often drops the articles of the, an and a. He uses short choppy sentences followed by long narrative ones in which he barely takes a breath. He forgets verbs, changes tense in the middle of a sentence and asks questions of the listener.

He will make you laugh and stir you with gut-wrenching sadness. Keeping the manuscript in his words may make for challenging reading, but once you get a feel for how he uses language, I believe you will agree that his story needed to be told in his voice with his point of view.

...

Copyright @ 2013 by Martha Rose Woodward, writer. Phillip Lim, writer. All rights reserved under International and Pan-American Copyright Conventions. Published in the United States of America CreateSpace in Charleston, S.C. and Seattle, WA. No portion of this book may be reproduced, stored in a retrieval system, or transmitted in any form or by any means, electronic, mechanical, photocopying, recording, used in a college or university class as a textbook, or otherwise, without the permission of the writers. Contact Sunspherebook @ aol.com. Book formatted for printing by graphic artist, Patricia Griffeth.

History book-non-fiction, biography, local history, Phillip Lim, Phillip Lim's history, Lim Lian Keng's history, Knoxville history, Asia Café Restaurant, Martha Rose Woodward, Martha Woodward, Knoxville, Tennessee, Malaysian history, Go Bananas Restaurant, Martha Sunsphere, MarthaSunsphere.blogspot.com, Louise Lim, Gary Lim, Jimmy Lim, Arthur Lim, David Lim, Shawn Lim, Heather Lim, Heidi Lim, Lim Soon, George Lim, Johnny Cash, Rita Cash, Sarah Shicks, Desiree Baker, Melaka, Malaysia, RR Chelvrajah, Sua Ah Jee, Richard Lim Cheng Ann, The Knoxville Journal Newspaper, Lim Keng, Bio-Vital, 6714 B N. Central Avenue, Knoxville, Tennessee, rubber tapping, Singapore, Cheng Hoon Teng Temple, Ouja board, map of Malaysia, Chinese history 1890s

Dedication

This book is dedicated to Louise Lim for her support and encouragement. Also, her eagle-eye editing allowed us to make a much better book.

I will begin the story of how I became an American businessman. It began with the decision of my great-grandfather, the great Lim Lian Keng to escape from a harsh style of leadership and poverty.

My great-grandfather was in a boat-a boat called a sampan. He came from Fukien, China in 1899 with his first son, Lim Sian Soon.

He traveled days and nights, days and nights to escape the brutality of those who were in charge in China. After about 60 days, they landed in Malacca, Malaysia, and of the 16 who began the journey, only 6 people survived. One was my great-grandfather. One was his son.

Great-grandfather left China to find opportunity. At the time, the leadership was very, very strong. You can not do anything except follow the government's rule. So he wanted to leave and find freedom. To find opportunity.

**Lim Keng, Phillip's great-grandfather
Born 1860 Died 1918**

Chapter One

My story begins…

This is my story. The story of an international businessman firmly grounded in American soil, whose roots are buried deeply in the darkness of war-torn China and poverty, and whose branches bear the fruit of both love of family and fabulous riches.

My name is Phillip. A man who was raised in great wealth, but one who did not know the value of money. It became necessary for my family to send me away from the safety of comfortable nest to fly into the world. I had to determine how to capture my own character and discover my abilities. I had to learn how to build my own nest.

Have you ever met anyone who went from riches to rags in order to find how to make it back to riches? Probably not. This is me. My own story is quite different from great-grandfather's. He escaped to freedom and turned the opportunity into riches. I was born into wealth, but had to learn the value of money.

I was born in Melaka, Malaysia in 1957, the second son of Richard Lim Cheng Ann and his first wife, Low Bok Neo, aka Sua Ah Jee. Their marriage was arranged when they were youngsters; both were born in Malacca, Malaysia (spelling changed to Melaka in 1946). Their marriage was successful producing seven children. My father, Richard Lim Cheng Ann, was the number three son of Lim Wah Mooi, my Chinese grandfather, who was born in 1909, and his third wife who was from Malacca, Malaysia.

I became the man that I am today-successful businessman, inventor, husband, father and friend by trial and error. My metamorphous spanned three continents, three wives, over twenty jobs and two religions.

However, none of us would have been born into freedom without the decision made by my great-grandfather, Lim Keng, in 1899 to board a sampan-a small fishing boat-with 15 other men and escape from the brutality in China by sailing to Malacca, Malaysia. One of the men who escaped with Lim Keng was Lim Sian Soon, his son, who was born fully Chinese from both Chinese father and mother.

So, here goes-the story of Phillip Boon Lim-all possible because my great-grandfather left China. He escaped to riches. As I tell my story, I will try to not embarrass myself. ***That may be impossible.***

**Phillip's grandfather Lim Wah Mooi
1909 to 1984**

Grandfather taught us to always dress your best; present yourself well. Others are judging you by your style, cleanliness and attention to detail. If you do not care for your body enough to dress well, you will not take care in business.

Another message passed down to me that I follow daily was to form the habits of taking showers each morning and each night. A shower at night allows you to wash away the bad things of the day-the problems, the dirt, the conflicts and no one should go to bed dirty. A shower each morning allows you to leave the house each day clean and fresh ready to begin a new day refreshed and in a good mood.

Chapter Two

Regular guy has big life.

In many ways I am a regular guy. If you saw me on the street you would probably think I look Asian. You might guess that I am from China or another country in the Far East.

In the years that I have lived on this earth, I have resided in Asia, Australia and North America. I have worked as class monitor, secretary to Chinese gang, office boy, stock boy, aide, store clerk, errand boy, driver, insurance salesman, factory worker, bus boy, dish washer, waiter, cook, advisor, electronics salesman, businessman, inventor, entrepreneur and restaurateur.

Let me say here that I am fully Americanized. Live in traditional American house on quiet street in upscale neighborhood. Drive Mercedes, attend Temple Baptist Church, cheer for UT Vols, sing karaoke and enjoy current fashions, gadgets, and gizmos sold in this country.

Like my great-grandfather and father before me, I have been married three times to three very different kinds of women . It took me a while, but finally found my soul mate. My third wife, Louise, good wife. She is responsible. My first two wives not good wives, not responsible. Second wife-terrible wife. You will hear all about that, too, if you read on. I have four children. Three that I fathered and one that I adopted. My children are beautiful. My reason for living. My joy. The Lim name continues.

If we met and had conversations, you would notice that I have heavy Chinese accent. But, mostly, I am typical citizen having no special looks, mannerisms or unusual qualities that separate me from others of ethic heritage.

However, if you continue to read my story, you will discover I have lived a remarkable life. In all ways, it has been like ride on very high, very fast rollercoaster. I climbed to the top, up, up, up; I fell just as quickly to the bottom and crashed only to ride back to the top, up, up, up; even higher. This pattern I have repeated many times. Oh, what ride it has been.

So, I grew up in a very strange way. You would think that the Chinese come from China have Chinaman mentality, not so in my family. My grandfather studied

English and graduated from Cambridge. My father from Harvard Business School.

We speak English; that is good news.

Phillip Lim in front of his restaurant, Asia Cafe.

It is a multiracial nation in Malaysia including people of many ethnic groups- Malaysians, Chinese, Indians, and others. Not Indians with cowboys, but from country of India. The national religion is Islam, however, tolerance to all religions is required. There are approximately 28% Catholics living in Malaysia, many Christians from other beliefs. My family are Buddhists. My current wife is Catholic.

I was raised very well. My family are industrialists. I was always given all the money I want. When I ask for money, I get it. In that town, when you mention the names, Lim Keng, or Lim Wah Mooi, you get what you want.

It was my grandfather's idea that the name Lim be carried down through the generations. He had three wives. His father had three wives. I have have been married three times. This makes for a lot of children. At one time my grandfather's children gave him grandchildren at the same time his brother's children had kids. I have many uncles and cousins in the same age range.

After completing high school in Melaka, Malaysia, I went to Melbourne, Australia to get bachelor's degree in business marketing. My family pay for everything, No problem.

Education top priority in Lim family. Grandfather, Lim Wah Mooi, often say,

"Without an education if anyone of us landed in the desert, we would not know how to find the directions of north, south, east, or west. We would not know how to follow the sun to see where the sun sets. Knowing where the sun sets is how we would find the path to palm trees and with trees there will be water."

As young man, I was spoiled brat. Liked to party. Liked spending time with cabaret girls. Liked to be in bars and in dance clubs.

After completing college I had opportunity to travel to Hong Kong. Exciting city; lots to do. Many things to see. Many ways to spend money. Went to bank and told banker, I am grandson of Lim Wah Mooi. Great-grandfather, Lim Keng. I told him, "I need money." Banker eagerly give me all the money I want. Banker is kin to Lim Sian Soon, son of my great-grandfather. I borrow $10,000. I use the money to go to night clubs like my grandfather. I pay for cabaret parties like my grandfather. I spend on party for self and pals. I provide exotic foods, gambling, booze and pretty girls. I am the fun guy. I organize great parties.

However, money comes due; I have no way to pay. Bank phones grandfather asking for $10,000 his grandson has borrowed. He picks up the phone. He answers the call. He is surprised. He pays for it; he likes me really well. He not happy with me, however.

I was what you call rascal. I party a lot. I watch TV. We rich. We have TV. I watch all I want to. Only black and white TV in those days.

I watch American cowboy and Indian shows. Gunsmoke, Lone Ranger, Big Valley, Bonanza. I fell in love with cowboys and Indians. I love Hoss Cartwright, John Wayne, Clint Eastwood, Marshall Matt Dillon-wow, I think, those guys were cool.

As I watch those TV shows, I stand in front of mirror and pretend to be in gun fight. "Draw," I say, and I pull my invisible pistol from the invisible gun holster belted around my hips. "Bang, you are dead," I yell at invisible bad guy who is wearing a black hat. I have great fun. My hat is white, of course.

I begin to dream of traveling to America. I want to be a cowboy. Can see myself wearing boots, riding on a horse and being a gunslinger. Wanted girls to dance Can-Can dance for me, too. I'd be a cool dude.

At night I sit in the yard at our home in Malaysia and stare up into the sky full of stars. I wonder, are these the same stars cowboys on the prairie are looking at tonight? My mind is lost in the dream of cowboys, Indians, boots, spurs, horses and saddles, Can-Can girls dancing with me because I am the best fighter, the fastest draw in the West. I gave no thought to how I was going to support myself in my quest to be fastest draw in the West. I did not know the value of money.

**Phillip's grandmother:
Wee Hye Choo Neo, born 1913
(date of death unknown)**

Chapter Three
ও঳ও঳ও঳

Survival skills are tested.

I have often wondered about courage of great-grandfather, honorable Lim Keng. What planning did it take for him to escape China? How long did he save money in order to pay for passage out of China? What conversations did he have with those who escaped with him? What must it have been like to embrace wife he loved so much for last time before boarding small sampan hoping to sail to freedom? How did he survive trip in vessel not meant for ocean travel with so many others on there with him? What did they do for food? How did they protect themselves from relentless rays of hot sun beating down day after day? How 'bout seasickness? Boat go up and down, up and down.

I wondered about the navigation of the trip. We know great-grandfather and Lim Soon, his son, paid for their passage on fishing boat. Did the man they paid for passage on vessel understand how to travel across ocean using stars as his guide? Had he made this trip before? Did he think he knew the way? Did he survive trip, too?

When we look at map and trace journey from Fukien, China to Melaka, Malaysia, it is not straight trip. Many places sampan could have landed before settling on Melaka's port. Does this mean man who steered ship knew where he was headed or was sampan adrift more days than needed in a relentless search for land?

I wondered about deaths of 10 who did not make it to Melaka. Of 16 who sailed on sampan, why did only 6 survive?

We know that sampan is, traditionally, small fishing boat, fourteen to sixteen feet in length. Sampans are not built or known for use in ocean travel. With 16 aboard, vessel was crowded. Men took turns to sleep, to help steer boat, to pull and push paddles, to work with boat's sails, to fish by dragging fish nets.

Fish would have been main source of food. Fish nets full of fish; all eat. Do not catch fish; all go hungry. Must believe men not catch enough fish as many died from starvation. Others said to have died from dehydration.

What did survivors do with dead bodies?

In Chinese culture, ancestors are extremely important. What can be said of family whose ancestor became nothing more than food for fishes?

In quiet moments such as cold, winter day when wind blows through hair, I have dared to think unspeakable? Could dead bodies have been used for food for more than fishes?

Just how hungry would men have to be to become cannibals? Would men who survived long trip turn to cannibalism? Would great-grandfather eat flesh of dead person?

We know from other events in history that cannibalism was used as last resort by people suffering through famines.

I once read about story from 1846. Ill-fated, Westward expedition of 87 people in Donner Party who were caught in heavy snowstorm in Nevada. Diary found described eating dogs, horses, then people who were dead. Some people in Donner Party may have killed children and cooked them.

I also once watched movie about crash of Uruguayan Air Force Flight 571 in 1972. Plane that was carrying members of Uruguayan rugby team, their friends and family. Group totaled 45. Of 14 who survived crash, only choices for food were some chocolate bars and wine. These didn't last long. Survivors made tough decision to eat flesh of dead passengers. When two survivors walked to get help, world was shocked that group was discovered alive after 72 days on snow-covered mountaintop. World more shocked when learned survivors became cannibals. Story of their survival inspired 1993 film Alive.

Cannibalism is topic we do not want to think about. However, if you have risked everything to get to freedom, what else would you be willing to do to survive?

We know, for centuries, people in the Chinese culture have eaten dogs, rats, snakes, spiders, and various internal organs from these animals as well as from pigs and cows. How different would it seem in mind of starving person to eat liver of dead man than liver of cow or pig?

These are questions that I turn over and over in my mind, but there is no one still alive that I can ask about this. I feel certain my great-grandfather would not want to talk about it, and what difference does it make anyway?

Great Lim Keng of China did what he had to do to escape and gain his freedom. He reached his goal and built family that continues to grow and prosper. He built much more than family and we will get to that as story progresses.

I am proud descendent of Lim Keng of Fukien, China, who escaped to freedom by sailing to Malaysia. I would have been nothing without courage, bravery and brilliance of great man.

We know that great-grandfather, Lim Keng, had three wives and two mistresses. He left Wife #1 in China and we do not know why she did not make the passage to Malaysia. He promised to return to China for #1 wife he left behind.

This was promise he could never keep.

People have often asked me, "Phillip, why didn't Lim Keng send to China for Wife #1?" I answer, People do not understand what it is like to live under harsh government in those days. Oh boy, no one sends to China to tell the government what to do.

For one thing, he didn't want those who were ruling China to know where he landed. He didn't want anyone to search for him and force him back to China to imprisonment. Lim Keng knew that number one wife was probably beaten and, possibly even killed when rulers saw that he and his son had escaped. This was way of the government, to kill family members when other members of family won victory over them.

Escaping to Melaka was victory Lim Keng won over government. He would not be rewarded for it.

There is not much known about great-grandfather's second wife. We know that he married her in Melaka, Malaysia. She was Muslim. We think they had no children.

Wife number three, Tan Swee Suan Neo, was also from Melaka, also Muslim and was mother to my grandfather, Lim Wah Mooi. All together great-grandfather had many children and even more grandchildren. It is not possible to know the exact count because records are not kept of mistresses.

My uncle, George Cheng Hock Lim, age 58, resident of Malaysia, continues to operate the Lim Keng Enterprises to this date and is the CEO. George is married to Dorene and has two sons, one daughter, and is a grandfather. George and I have the same grandfather.

He reports that Lim Keng had six children; four boys and two girls. The girls married and raised families. The first son was fully Chinese and traveled on the sampan with Keng. One of the boys went into government service, one was a banker and one worked for the family business which morphed into becoming a general insurance company and barters (exporters and importers) for spices. Barters are also known as traders.

George also tells us that, at one point, Lim Keng was an arms and ammunitions dealer. During Keng's life span-1860 until 1918, there were only two arms dealers in Malaysia, Lim Keng being one. Both Lim Keng and Lim Sian Soon were involved in the political undertones surrounding the rights afforded to Chinese immigrants to Malaysia. To speak further of their activities would open a big can of worms with national and international repercussions. Suffice to say that their efforts lay the groundwork for the founding of the new Malaysia that occurred in 1957.

Malaysian historians know of civil disturbances between Chinese and Malay gangsters that caused political unrest that nearly overthrew the Malaysian government My relatives were heavily involved in the movement of these Chinese gangs and probably sold them arms and ammunitions.

The land owned by Lim Keng and Lim Sian Soon once occupied by their latex reprocessing factory was donated for the purpose of building other structures for the Cheng Hoon Teng Temple. It was said to be worth over $2 million dollars.

Lim Wah Mooi and Wee Hye Choo Neo
(married at age 16)

This information was taken from family documents:
Grandfather Lim Wah Mooi 1909-1984

Married Wife in 1925:
Madam Wee Hye Choo Neo-
born 1913-(date of death unknown)
Born into this marriage
5 children: 4 boys; I girl
Lim Cheng Chwee-1930-male
Lim Cheng Chye-1933-male
Lim Cheng Ann-1935 (also known as Richard)-male
Lim Kiat Yam Neo-1936 (female)
Lim Cheng Kee-1941-male

2nd Wife-name not known-no children

Married Madam Liau Ah Moi
born 1935 (date of marriage and her death not known)
Born into this marriage
4 children: 2 boys; 2 girls
George Lim Cheng Hock 1956-male
Henry Lim Cheng Hee 1958-male
Jenny Lim Kiat Bee 1960-female
Helen Lim Kiat Hun 1962-female

Chapter Four

More about great-grandfather

Lim Lian Keng was born in Fukien, China in 1860. We know he escaped China on sampan in 1899. The only item he brought with him was wooden pillow.* We know he was 39 years old when he made that faithful trip. His first son, Lim Sian Soon was also aboard the sampan and survived the trip.

We also know that his son, Lim Wah Mooi, was born in 1909 in Melaka, Malaysia to his third wife who was from Melaka, Malaysia. Although Lim Keng was Chinese and practiced Confucius-style Buddhism, wives were Muslims.

We know what he looked like as a well-worn photograph of him continue to hang on the wall of the house he purchased. Family members continue to live in this house and will always have permission to do so.

All offspring of Lim Keng are mixed breed having Chinese from their father and Malaysian from their mothers. In Malaysian culture, children of mixed marriages are known as nyonyas-girls and babas- boys. I myself am baba.

According to tales handed down in words, when sampan carrying Keng landed in port in Melaka, he and his son were in bad shape physically. He described himself as being near death saying he was starving, was thirsty. Lips parched. Tongue swollen. Signs of dehydration. Skin brown and leathery like an old shoe. Black hair burned deep bronze with blonde streaks having had no protection from the rays of the sun. Eyes swollen and crusted with salt blown onto him by harsh ocean winds. He could barely walk and was carried from boat by curious onlookers who spotted sampan on the distant horizon headed to island miles before it landed. Great-grandfather was probably hauled inland on board oxen cart.

People near shore that day thought they were looking at ghosts. They were shadowy figures, maybe not live men. Malaysians cared for great-grandfather, his son and four other survivors by hauling them off of sad-looking boat, giving them water, food and place to stay until they had recovered from arduous journey. Great-grandfather probably bedded down in shed with oxen and felt lucky to do so. Possibly fed oxen and shoveled dung from barns or sheds in trade for opportunity to sleep in straw near animals.

Lim Keng regained health in few weeks. It was suggested he could possibly get job working as tapper on rubber plantation. He did.

What must it have seemed like to him when he first glimpsed the majestic rubber trees in green, tropical, forests that surrounded town?

Tall rubber trees having holes punched in tree bark take on characteristics of giant sized men with big, black, sunken eyes.

What did great-grandfather think of palm trees with large prongs blowing in winds seeming to reach for sky? Of fruits such as bananas, mangos, papayas and berries growing near streets? All man had to do was reach and pick fruit to eat. In such a land, he knew, he never go hungry again.

A rubber tapper is worker who takes raw latex from tall rubber trees. First, bark is removed from trees in specific way with use of rather odd looking knife. Next, worker cuts hole or large gash in side of tree with knife that looks more like what Americans would see as a windshield scraper. Knife's blade runs up and down, not sideways. Hook on end of knife aids in scraping motion. Next step-placing bucket or pan under white liquid or fluid that flows out. Once bucket is full, sticky contents are transferred to vat or large basin.

Next, when full, huge basin is lifted onto wagon or ox cart and hauled to factory.

Great-grandfather worked as tapper in green forest cutting bark on tall trees in exact circular way in order for white latex to follow path and drip into buckets.

Work in massive forest began early in morning before tropical heat became suffocating. Hot sun was relentless. Temperatures rose to 90s, even 100s. Only relief from conditions of climate came from patches of shade provided under tall trees and during long wagon rides delivering latex to rubber factory. Heavy rains caused moderate drop in temperatures. Also brought muggy humidity.

Much work was done late into night when temperatures were cooler.

Perhaps there was time to grab quick nap huddled under ox cart or in patches of shade under tall, green trees when temperatures rose in midday or when rain fell. The flow of latex sap stopped near midday to workers' delight.

Tasks were repetitive and never ending. Lim Keng worked hard and taught himself to focus on future and to think about his dreams. Rubber plantation full of workers. Each person did job and did it well. Constant tapping or pinging of hammers rang out echoing throughout majestic trees. Sounds of extractions were sounds of wealth flowing from tall trees.

Learning to focus on task at hand was life skill great-grandfather learned traveling on sampan for 60 days when crossing ocean. He learned necessity of working hard and value of money on rubber plantation. He saw ways of making his life better and he grabbed them.

These were skills he taught his sons and grandsons. Men in my family would often point to photograph of great-grandfather on the wall and say, "Focus on what you want to do and, eventually, you will do it." These are words handed down through oral history.

Lim Keng left China because he dreamed of freedom. Once he was free, his dream changed while he was working as tapper on rubber plantation.

Each tap, each bucket full of latex, brought him closer to his new dream - to take advantage of opportunities and to amass great wealth.

He must have been an observant man who noticed owner of plantation driven to site by chauffeurs in expensive buggies. He must have taken note when owner walked to and fro dressed in finery and possessing power to order men around. Owner wore shoes, something not possible for lowly rubber tappers. Owner kept company with beautiful women, something else not possible for poor man. He must have asked, "Why not me?"

Lim Keng learned first-hand differences of life for rubber tappers and for those who have wealth and power. Seed of desire for finer things in life was planted in heart of lowly rubber tapper. He must have secretly plotted in his mind that he would some day wear expensive suits, feel what it was like to pull shoes and socks onto his feet, eat fat ducks, drink his fill of coconut juice and enjoy companionship of beautiful women.

He must have spent hours thinking about what he must do in order to make his dreams come true. Tap; flow; tap; flow. His mind must have been working while his body performed repetitive tasks.

He clearly saw, money was key; money bought land and with land came power.

He would need to save money to achieve success he craved. He purposed in his heart that he would learn everything he needed in order to become rich like plantation owners he observed dressed in tailor-made suits of linen or wool, keeping companionship of beautiful women dressed in soft silks dripping with jade earrings, having well-nourished children chewing on chunks of fresh coconut or pineapple at his side day to day.

He would have it all. He would make a better life for himself.

It took many years, but he did it. He became man who arrived driven in buggy by chauffeur, barking orders at foremen and lowly workers. Arriving with beautiful woman by his side and plenty of children to continue his legacy.

While other workers spent meager wages on bad women and booze, Lim Keng saved money. By focusing on goals, he was soon able to take first step up ladder to success.

He was wise to figure it out. Land was key. Land was way to gain money and power. Even though it seemed impossible and it was improbable, he was soon able to buy small piece of property.

He used land wisely. Rented small piece of property to another businessman who needed space in good location in town to conduct business. Keng began collecting rent money. By continuing to save money from his own wages and from rental income, he was soon able to buy more land.

Within few years, Lim Keng bought small rubber processing factory. He went into business processing rubber extracted from plantation he had worked on when tapper. The observant student solved puzzle and walked through the maze on his journey up the ladder of success.

Imagine how self-satisfied Lim Keng must have felt when he went into business with people who hired him to do most meager of tasks? While others may have rested or spent time doing nothing of merit, he studied rubber business from most basic point - tapping trees. As if he were following stepping stones, he learned each procedure needed in order to turn the raw latex into a product ready for exportation.

Son Lim Soon, who survived trip from China, also became part of great-grandfather's dream. They worked along side of each other while planning for their futures.

They went into business together; both becoming rich. At the times of their deaths, both were millionaires. In today's dollars, they would have been multimillionaires.

I worked for my grandfather's companies name of Lim Keng. They have this name as their corporation. Like Trump or Gates of his time period. Still today, Lim

Keng Enterprises are operating. Legacy is there; name did not die off. Original factory was torn down to make room to build annex to temple.

What did Lim Keng value? I think he value upbringing children. Values taught by Lim Keng handed down to my grandfather and father: work, save money, always better yourself and family is everything.

*According to Wikipedia: "Traditional Chinese pillows are often hard boxes made from stone, wood, metal, or porcelain instead of stuffed fabric."

Traditional Chinese Pillow

Louise, Phillip and their grandson Hayden in 2011.

Melaka River, Malaysia (photo by Gary Lim)

Chapter Five
ಒಬಒಬ

Melaka, Malaysia in the 1890s

In order to better understand great-grandfather Lim Keng's, decision to escape China and travel to Melaka, Malaysia, brief look at history of time period helpful.

History provided by web site for Malaysia tells us that many Chinese workers traveled to Malaysia to work in tin mines and on rubber plantations during 1800s. Some say, "Massive migration."

Were workers who left China bought and sold as slaves? Were they lured to Malaysia by traders who promised riches? Were some allowed to leave China on their own? Did others buy their way into indentured servitude?

We will never know full answers to these questions, but we can assume that each of these things happened along with other possibilities.

We know history of Melaka, Malaysia is tied to history of British Empire and to travels of Dutch explorers who found items to export from region. Rubber, tin, exotic fruits, wild pigs, oxen, spices and more. Greedy traders were hell bent on plundering natural resources found in abundant on island that had been ignored for centuries by traders. Europeans were willing and anxious to buy ship loads of bounty. Supply could not keep up with demand.

British East India Company, who partly controlled India, became India's important trade partner in late 18th century. At that time, British East India Company began looking for base in Malaysia. In 1786, British occupied Penang and founded Georgetown led by Francis Light. Province Wellesley came under their control in 1800.

In 1824, Treaty of London divided region between British and Dutch. Deal was struck giving British control of Melaka and Dutch control of Sumatra and all area below Malay Peninsula. Many hands in pot and plenty for all to share. Those with interests and others out of greed decided to divide bounty and move on with the plundering.

With influx of workers from China and India, the Straits Settlements - Penang, Province Wellesley, Melaka and Singapore- steadily grew in population. Although British East India Company controlled islands and parts of coast, they did not control interior of Malay Peninsula. In 1867, entire area was made a crown colony.

By this time, tin and rubber were major exports as news spread of vast riches available from exporting these items. Trade was brisk and hungry mouths of bankers, industrialists and fortune seekers could not be satisfied. Massive amount of workers were needed to do tedious, back-breaking work in mines and rubber tree forests. Opportunities abounded for poor, under class to be exploited. If not considered slaves, few freedoms were available to them. Was this great-grandfather's plight?

In 1853, British government decided to stop charging duty on imports on tin. Result, exports of tin from Malaya to Britain skyrocketed making many lucky businessmen filthy rich in process. Oh, Lordy, to be man in line to benefit from this decision.

Fortunes were made seemingly overnight by those with head to see direction of prevailing winds. Steamships speeding through waterways as water power turned turbines. Opening of Suez Canal in 1869 further boosted exports of tin. Chinese workers flocked to work in tin mines of Malaysia and on plantations as rubber tappers. Products could now be transported even more quickly to awaiting markets. It was as if money, not rubber, was growing on trees. What time to be alive!

It is possible that great-grandfather had heard of need for workers in tin mines and on rubber plantations in Malaysia. Was this why risk his life to escape to freedom on sampan with fifteen other men? Recorded facts of history are congruent with great-grandfather's story.

Clock tower installed by Dutch in Melaka in 1799.
Photo by Gary Lim 2013.

Chapter Six

Grandfather Lim Wah Mooi and grandmother Wee Choo Hye Neo
Father Richard Lim Cheng Ann and Mother Sua Ah Jee also known as Low Bok Neo

The child of Lim Keng most important to me, of course, is my grandfather, Lim Wah Mooi, born in 1909. He had three wives, two mistresses; second mistress had children, but only one is half-brother to my dad. I think he had sixteen grandchildren.

It was my grandfather's desire that the name Lim be brought down to our next generation. He made suggestion that each member of family who was born in same generation -my generation-the third generation from great-grandfather Lim Keng, keep name of Lim.

This is typical for the way things are done in USA, also British way. We follow grandfather's desire and keep name of Lim. We can be identified by it. The name connects us to Lim Keng, the first generation from China to Malaysia.

The death of my grandfather was one of the saddest times in my life. He was everything to me and I to him. What would I do without him in my life? His love. His approval. His wise counsel.

It is the custom in Malaysia when there is a death, they leave the coffin out for five days. In those five days the priest will walk around the coffin and say and do specific things. The family walks around the coffin and also says and does specific things. Many things are done to honor the deceased. An altar is built. Flowers are placed on altar. Incense is burnt. Prayers are said. There is music. It is the way we show our grief.

We gather with family and friends and eat certain foods. A priest gives a message about the dead person. The family pays the temple and the priest for the ceremony. People send flowers. There is big celebration. The richer the person is who dies, the bigger the party or celebration. There can be a live band playing music. Many families can not afford such celebrations. Only the rich can afford the activities like the one held for my grandfather.

After five days, the body is cremated.

When my grandfather died, the men in the family-my father, myself, my uncle and my father's sister's husband went to the cremation. It was held late at night-almost midnight after the celebration of the funeral was over.

The cremation took place outside, but everyone had gone home but us. As we stood watching the body burn, the four of us saw people standing next to us. We did not know these people.

We asked them, "What are you doing here?" But they gave no answers. We think they were ghosts.

I believe that my grandfather's soul came up during the cremation and these spirits greeted him. They take him to the other world. We turned and these people were gone.

We were a little bit afraid.

The next day we told other family members and they laughed at us. But it was true; it was real. I believe it.

I have seen a lot in the spirit world in my lifetime. If you ask me to go to a haunted place, I will see ghosts. I am not afraid. On several occasions I see ghosts and hear spirits when I am alone. I have no fear. I know these are ghosts of ancestors.

**Phillip's parents:
Richard Lim Cheng Ann and Sua Ah Jee,**
also known as Low Bok Neo

Richard Lim Cheng Ann is born in 1935 in Melaka, Malaysia. After completing college, he went into the car sales, and into import and export business involving heavy machinery. Father also dabbled in politics. All family were and are industrialists and entrepreneurs.

Half-brother still alive; my uncle die; my father die in 2006. My father is the son who took most after great-grandfather.

My father, number three son of Lim Wah Mooi, fathered five sons; two daughters. Gary, first son born 1956; next was Phillip born 1957; then, twin sisters Margaret and Annie born 1958, Arthur born 1959; Jimmy born 1960; and David born 1962. Why a year was skipped between 1960 and 1962? My mother had a miscarriage in 1961. Sister Annie passed away in 2009.

My mother, Low Bok Neo, also known as Sua Ah Jee, is still alive. She is number one wife of my father. She is born in 1938 in Melaka. She was adopted by a very wealthy family when she was nine years old and made to do their household chores. Mother continues to live in house in Melaka, Malaysia, purchased by Lim Keng. She may do so all her life. Margaret lives with her.

The marriage between my father and mother was arranged when they were nine years old. This was the tradition in those times; it was done to keep the wealth within the families. Arranged marriages can seem like a life sentence into unhappiness, however, for my parents it worked. They remained deeply in love until my father's death in 2006.

Children and grandchildren of great Lim Keng were raised with abundance, having nice houses, servants to wait on us hand and foot. Chauffeurs to drive us to and from school and other places we needed or wanted to go. We had finest clothes, foods, jewels, cars - anything our hearts desired. We were rich kids. Our friends were rich kids, too.

So, this is how it was and is with the generations. The ones who came before us did the hard work, made the sacrifices in order for their children to have abundance. We must not waste it.

Bandhar Hilir Primary School, Melaka, Malaysia.

Phillip Lim in front of Asia Cafe in 2013.

Chapter Seven

I accept the mantle that has been passed down to me.

Lim Lian Keng never forgot that he came from China. He wanted name Lim to be carried down to each generation of his family. To ensure his dynasty, Lim Keng married three wives who born him children and grandchildren.

Great-grandfather also became extremely wealthy. I have explained how he got his start. This wealth afforded him luxury of taking two mistresses; something that was culturally accepted in 1800's Malaysia. He was known as excellent businessman and one who loved entertainment.

We spent much of our teenage years having elaborate parties. Word "party" describes 40 to 60 young people, dressed in finery, eating most tasty foods, drinking whiskey, wine, or beer, and dancing. Culture of 1960s allowed our excesses; we eagerly partook.

Do you ask, Phillip, why do you speak so much about Lim Keng? His story is an old one; happened long time ago. Why all this to do about an old man dead and in his grave many years ago? I will answer. I believe the spirit of Lim Keng has been passed down to me.

From religious studies we learn the term, "taking up the mantle." This occurs when an individual dies and life's work is given over to next person chosen to continue path. By taking up mantle, an individual has, in a formal way, accepted certain duties or important job of carrying family legacy.

The mantle was often seen as a symbol of a person's willingness to sacrifice or make commitment to keep ways of ancestors. In earliest years, it was actual garment. A cloak. We might call cloak an overcoat.

Time passed, world spun around many times and taking up mantle came to be symbolic, not actually putting on clothes from deceased person. The mantle showed power and authority to assume the role of person who died.

Christians believe that taking up the mantle could mean that an individual is carrying forward with the message from God. The mantle could be a man's gift, the call given by God, and purpose for which God has called him the believer.

Every believer has a spiritual gift. Some have many gifts. The gift or gifts are given by God to assist each person to do in your life what God's plan is for your life.

In the Malaysian culture, the mantle would ordinarily fall on shoulders of the first son. However, it is my belief that the mantle of Lim Keng, to carry on with his story- to not let it die- has been placed with me.

I am son who has passion for telling the story of Lim Keng's journey. The escape from oppression. Sixty days in a sampan sailing on the ocean to an unknown land. The rise from lowly rubber tapper to millionaire.

Although my brothers have appreciation for the story, keeping the memory alive, making it vivid, has settled in my heart; I must do this. I can not get away from it. I must tell Lim Keng's story. I claim Lim Keng's mantle.

The story of Lim Keng is closely tied into the story of our homeland, too. My family vividly remembers living through the unrest. There were nights of strange sounds in the air, shouting, feet pounding on the earth, cracks and booms from firecrackers or was it gunfire

Malaysia declared independence from British rule on August 31, 1957. But, the work of figuring out a way to blend the various mix of people from many races and cultures, and uniting them under a common flag was difficult.

When the agreement was done, the newly written constitution spread the power into thirds-Malays, Indians, and Chinese. Three men are given title as founders: Tun Tan Cheng Lock-Chinese, who is my mother's father's first wife's uncle, Tun Sambantan-Indian, and Tunku Abdul Rahman-Muslim and a member of royalty.

Tun Tan Cheng Lock's son, is Tun Tan Siew Sin, Minister of Finance; more connections to my family. Do you notice the names Cheng and Lock? Both are my relatives. The spirit, the longing inside us to be free, to have opportunities is there. This lineage began in both sides of our family and continues.

During independence, Malays, who, after all, represented the majority of people living in the country, were given permanent spots in the government. Although there is a strong Catholic presence in the country, Islam was made the national religion. Malay was declared the national language, however, most people strive to learn English. The Chinese firmly dominated in the areas of business and trade, yet room has been made for others to share in this area.

At one point, the government controlled by the United Malay National Organization, passed the New Economic Policy, which attempted to increase economic opportunity for the Malay by establishing various quotas in their favor. Opposition arose from the Chinese, who quickly formed a significant opposition party. My relatives led in this fight.

Verbal battles have raged and tempers have flared over the years as melding the needs and wants of the mixture of groups having wildly different beliefs had led the country to developing an overall sense of tolerance. Clearly, the inhabitants of the island of Malaysia have major decision: duke it out or agree to disagree and move forward into the new world with a sense of purpose. Growth and abundance of business opportunities currently abounding in Malaysia are evidences that the choice has been made to develop tolerance. It could be said that living on island of Malaysia is like living on a boat; our successes, our prosperity or lack of it, sinks or swims with our ability to find middle ground; tolerance is name of the game. We come up or go down together. Most prefer to go up.

*Malaysia changed spelling of Malacca to Melaka after Malaysia got independence from the British in 1946.

Example of an altar built to honor ancestors.

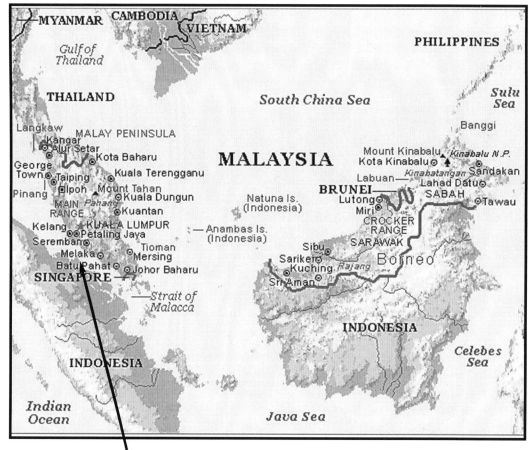

Melaka, Malaysia

"During my life I picked up the roots of great-grandfather Lim Keng. I have carried these roots forward and passed them on to future generations like a runner passing the torch in the Olympics." Phillip Lim

Chapter Eight

Rich kids growing up in Melaka in 1960s

What was it like to be rich kid growing up in Melaka, Malaysia in 1960s? Play a Beatles album and you will get the general idea.

My life was fabulous. I had everything child could ever want. Lived in very nice house with two sisters, four brothers. Were dressed in fine clothing. Nice shirts, good pants, leather shoes from best stores in town. Were driven to and from school by chauffeur in shiny new Mercedes. Not made to walk or ride in rickshaw.
Lady who cooked our meals was dressed in crisp, white dress. "Live-in" maid, dressed in black dress and white apron cleaned and did laundry. We spent leisure time at lavish parties. Played soccer, attended school and social events and were held in highest of esteem by parents and grandparents.

Each morning for breakfast-our cook served egg from fat duck, porridge-made from rice, or noodles and choice of fruits-pineapple, mango, banana, papaya. We drank tea. We could drink coconut milk, if desired. We had plenty to eat while many had nothing.

Lunches were eaten at school in cafeterias where tasty recipes were prepared on site by experienced cooks. Were served noodles, rice, always rice, plenty of vegetables, exotic fruits. The aromas of the hot spices and sizzling meats wafted throughout the classrooms and hallways. Cloves, cumin, ginger, white and black pepper, lemon grass, cinnamon-all smells that made our mouths water. We often ate pineapple tarts, banana pudding, oranges, mangos, papayas--fresh fruits or other baked goodies made for enjoyment.

Dinner always included meat-plump chickens, pork from fat pigs, beef from well-fed cattle-prepared in excellent manner. Recipes developed by mixing ingredients brought to Melaka by various cultures throughout the years were in daily use. Fresh vegetables sprinkled with a variety of spices were a must. The aromas drifting into air made us edgy with anticipation for meal we were about to enjoy.

Meals not prepared by our family's personal cooks were made by my mother and grandmother; most often by my grandmother. They do not think about how one day these recipes will become a valuable commodity for us to use in our restaurant, The Asia Cafe. They just cooked and were happy to make us feel full and smile.

Recipes of theirs I use are traditional. Asian food is best when served hot-very hot. Right now, in my restaurant, I will say of the recipes from my family, Shrimp Laksa is my most popular dish. The spices are hot and very good. Satay is an appetizer that comes on a skewer-on a stick-people love it. Beef Rendang is considered as an exotic food. It is also native food to Malaysia.

Serving a whole Spring chicken became so famous in Melaka, Malaysia that "Lifestyles of the Rich and Famous," with Robin Leach, filmed in my former restaurant a few years ago.

My childhood world was filled with colorful flowers and lush tropical growth from palm trees abundant with coconuts that dropped to the earth without effort on our part. We lived near ponds and waterways of sparkling waters that created a prime tropical paradise that presented, and still continues to present, a wide variety of fish species in both inland and out in the ocean surrounding our country. It was common for local fisherman to pull boats full of tropical game fish including the marlin and sailfish from the tropical seas. Tuna, cobia, mackerel, dorado, barracuda, sharks and more--all plentiful and there for the taking.

My father owned fishing boats and had staff to man them. Fish big part of our lives. The smell of fresh fish evokes memories in my mind of dead fish eyes starring up at me from rows of fish resting on ice. Today, I see fish; I smell Melaka.

On drive to school, we passed gardens of dew sprinkled blossoms of deep red, bright yellow, orange, white, pink, lilac, purple and blue flowers such as hibiscus, lotus, frangipani, bougainvillea, orchids, fuchsia and others. Streets were lined with gigantic palm trees lush with growth of green prongs that swayed in the wind like skirts on very tall women.

We were born into a life aflame with natural colors in a mystical environment overflowing with plenty of everything requiring little, if any effort on our parts. The beauty and bounty of our lives mimicked the beauty and bounty of nature. It was as if our ancestors paved the streets and laid the bricks that built our futures.

At all times we were taught respect for our parents, meal time was no exception. We were trained to sit at table. We were not allowed to jump around and grab for spoons and gobble food like pigs eating slop. Made to wait for mother and father to sit down before we could begin meal.

Important part of parenting to Father and to Mother to be with their seven children for meals. Once parents were at table, we always asked them, "Father, Mother, may we eat now?" Parents pick up chop sticks and spoons and say, "Yes, you may begin. Eat now."

Food was there for each to share. No one greedy or took more than his/her share. Always made to ask, "Brother, Sister, would you care for food from my plate or bowl?"

We were trained with British manners and customs.

From kindergarten through 5th grade, I attended Siang Lin School. Siang Lin is private Chinese school for wealthy children in town. Throughout six years I spent in this school, I had plenty of friends. Was well-mannered, bright student who advanced in studies. It was often said, "Phillip handsome young man."

I was teacher's pet. I appear; teacher smile. Chosen as class monitor. Teacher visited our home and full of praises about me, my conduct, my abilities in my studies. Parents beamed with pride. Yes, I was golden child.

In kindergarten, I clearly remember participating in performance at a special event at school. It was one of those nights when parents are invited and children from each class provide the entertainment by singing, dancing, reciting poetry or showing some skills. I remember that I entertained the crowd by riding my tricycle all around stage. In my mind I can still see face of my happy mother who had taken care to dress me in snappy, new clothes for event. Shoes polished by rubbing them with blossoms of Bougainvillea. People in audience that night were smiling and clapping for me. I loved getting positive attention. Approval was as intoxicating as fragrance of flowers.

I remember feeling gleeful. I rode new tricycle. "Whee, whee," I said. Audience clapped and fawned over me, cute great-grandson of Lim Keng. I knew they were thinking, "He is wonderful son. Look at him, beautiful child, great-grandson of rich Lim Keng and grandson of Lim Wah Mooi, who is also rich."

During middle school years, I attended Gajah Berang Lin School. Each day I wore required uniform consisting of white shirt-must be pressed very good. Hate to have starch, but did sometimes. Kaiki colored, brown shorts, as did all students. Each day when arrived at school sharply at 8 a.m., we marched into large assembly hall, stood tall while sing national anthem of Malaysia.

Tap-tap-tap came over intercom. Next came sound of needle scratching on record played by record player. Horns would blow and song began:

Daa-da-da-da-da-da Daa-da-da-da-da-da

We would sing: Negaraku (My Country)
Negaraku (My country)
Tanah tumpahnya darahku (The land where my blood was spilt.)
Rakyat hidup, bersatu dan maju.(The people living united and progressive,)
Rahmat bahagia, Tuhan kurniakan, (May God bestow blessing and happiness,)
Raja kita, selamat bertakhta, (May our King have a successful reign.)
Rahmat bahagia, Tuhan kurniakan, (May God bestow blessing and happiness,)
Raga kita, selamat bertakhta. (May our King have a successful reign.)

Malaysian Flag

After singing, we took seats when given directions to do so.

School officials spoke to us each morning making announcements about upcoming events. Always, always reminding us to be respectful. Show obedience, complete our school work, and honor our elders.

Next, our classes were dismissed from assembly hall in specific order. Monitor called out names of teachers who were standing at back of room to greet us. Opening exercises for day never varied. We expected each thing to occur in same order; we needed and trusted consistency.

Everything was done in decent way and in order. Each class walked out of grand assembly room in single file form with military precision. No student dared to talk or to push his/her way in front of someone else. Each class walked quickly and quietly down long hallways to our rooms keeping single lines straight as arrows; none dared to step out of place or to even whisper single word.

After arriving at our classrooms, we took our places standing behind desks. We were greeted by classroom monitors who bossed us around. We did not sit down until our teacher arrived and monitor called name of teacher.

Monitor might say, "Attention class. Good morning, Mrs. Weng." Our class would answer in unison, "Good morning, Mrs. Weng." Teacher might say, "You may now be seated." Monitor would take seat in classroom at this time.

Thus began long days of sitting quietly on hard-bottomed, wooden desks, that were nailed to floors in straight rows.

School in those days was not like it is here in America. There was no talking back to teacher. There was no whispering to friends. We obeyed teachers and completed lessons.

We had excellent teachers. I never saw one slouching or resting. They were professionals who held our feet to fire as they guided us through the curricula. Kind of teachers who wrote on board with one hand while erasing and moving on with other hand. "Much to do," was motto of teachers.

Technique of discipline mostly used by teachers was to signal their disapproval or approval with use of their eyes. They rarely spoke about our behavior or production of our lessons-only using shake of head or raised eyebrows. If teacher closed eyes and let out deep breath, we knew something bad; something wrong. Do you think person can smile with eyes? I do. Teachers smiled with eyes when giving approval.

At one point, in teenage years, however, I began to rebel against authority. One time I stole book or some small object from another student. I do not remember exactly what I took. I do not know why I did this. I was rich kid. I had money in my pocket. I could buy any book or small object I wanted, but, I guess, it gave me quick thrill to steal something. Maybe I wanted to feel like big man; like I could make my own decisions. Maybe it was just a foolish prank.

My foolish choice was soon discovered. Everyone knew I was a good kid, but I was made to stand in front of classmates and apologize. Discipline had to be fair.

My teacher also ordered me to hold my arms out and to stretch my fingers out and to point palms of my hands towards ceiling. I obeyed teacher and wondered how I could have gotten myself into trouble. Everyone knew I was honest, not a thief.

Suddenly teacher took wooden ruler and whacked palm of my hand with sharp blow. Ouch, it hurt. Sound of smack bellowed through the room even out into the hallway. Everybody in room very quiet.

My hand stinging and burning, but teacher gave no time to recover. Smack, came second whack. I felt pain from blow surge like lightning all way up my arm. I took deep breath and swallowed hard. It was all I could do to keep tears from swelling up in eyes.

Thoughts were pouring through brain. Wasn't I favorite student of teachers? Wasn't I cute little boy who rode tricycle on stage while people clapped and cheered? Wasn't I rich grandson of Lim Wah Mooi who was held in highest esteem by everyone in town? Was I receiving punishment? Me, handsome son who had never been spanked or beaten. What in world was happening to me? How did I get into this situation? Names of ancestors no good now. Names could not help me.

These thoughts and more were quickly flashing through mind. I rubbed injured hand with other hand hoping pain would soon pass.

"Your hand," teacher ordered. "Oh no," I was thinking, but I knew rules. Discipline required three blows. I had seen other students receive punishment and, yes, I had giggled and joked with friends about it.

Pow, third whack came before I had time to blink. Stabbing pain in hand running up my arm was so fierce that tears popped out and fell from eyes. I had no control about it. Pain was excruciating. I had been a silly boy; disappointment to my family, to my school, and to myself. Now I suffered the consequence.

Sniffling with moisture pouring from my mouth and eyes, I walked back to desk wiping face and took my place among classmates. I put head down on desk and covered face to hide shame.

I knew that mother, father and grandfather would hear about my indiscretion and punishment before I would arrive back home that evening. I could see in my mind that they would stare in disbelief.

These thoughts were almost more than I could stand. Punishment of taking three hard whacks to hand had been bad, but seeing disapproval of my mother, father and grandfather would be much worse.

I resolved that I would face shame. I spent rest of day in school with dread in my heart. I resolved what I had to do. I would beg family for forgiveness. I would make solemn promise to them that I would never steal anything again, even as a silly joke.

I determined in my heart that I would never do anything to bring dishonor to proud family. I would never feel embarrassment of crying in front of classmates. I resolved that I would fly straight as arrow from this point forward.

Ride home in chauffeur-driven, shiny car was strangely quiet. Even chauffeur met me with scowl on his usually happy face. This told me that everyone had heard of my prank and punishment. When we arrived home, it was all I could do to walk into house, but I had to. There was no where to run. My mother was sitting in chair crying. My father was standing by her with his arm on back of chair. His eyes grew larger as I approached.

"Phillip, my son," he said. "We have heard about your situation at school today."

"Please forgive me," I begged and I hung my head. "I will not do anything like this again."

"Phillip, your mother and I love you. We do not, however, want you to break the rules at school. We know that you are an honest boy. We suspect that you were clowning around and the situation got out of your control. Go and wash you face and always remember that you have our love."

I turned to go and caught glimpse of my mother's eyes. Tears were running down her face. This made my heart ache. I held her gaze for as long as I could before turning and leaving room. How could I have been so stupid as to hurt my mother, such a kind and good lady, in this way? It was a lesson I would remember.

Life moved on from that point with the only other remarkable thing that happened to me during middle school was that I joined Chinese gang. You may wonder why I did this. I did it because I wanted people to think that I am tough. I do not want anyone to come and bother me. When you mentioned that you are with gangster's club, no one will mess with you.

I became Secretary to Chinese Temple-known as Gangster Temple. The Secretary is person who takes in money. Organizes shows for Chinese guards. I was never involved in crimes or anything like that. It was my way to be involved in life. It was what young men of my age did at the time. An entrance into adulthood.

Even then I was recognized as person with eye for business.

Gang members I knew was Chinese-Malaysian; a baba. They were Buddhists. They came to Chinese Temple to pray. They would do bad things, then pray. I kept track of money that was needed for shows and whatever else club required. I was honest and had good head for business. Gang members knew that grandson of Lim Wah Mooi and the son of Lim Cheng Ann could be trusted.

There is another world containing activity of Chinese gangs that I know about but am not at liberty to fully discuss. You do not think man who escaped brutalities in China arrived in Melaka riding on the unicorn with roses on his shoulders and rainbow shining in his face do you? How such a soft touch as this survive trip? He would not.

Lim Keng not soft touch. He what we can call "a tough cookie." He found a way to slip around and escape from most brutal of dictatorship. He brings those skills to Melaka with him. He quickly learned of the exploitation of Chinese immigrants by greedy Malays. This was something he fought against his entire life.

He not fight out in the open; that was not his way. You do not escape from captors by being out in open. You escape by whispering, by deciding who can be trusted, who cannot be trusted. You escape by watching, knowing how to read people, how to go and how to stay. He know how to store weapons, where to keep ammunition.

Lim Keng realized that getting arms and ammunition was a key to winning any battle. He knew preparation is the key. He sat about and made himself one of two arms dealers in the city at that time. The leadership skills he used and the secrets he kept propelled the unified Chinese to point of nearly overthrowing Malays. It's a wonder he survived, but survival was his specialty.

My involvement with gangsters became source of sore spot for son of Lim Keng, grandfather Lim Wah Mooi. There was a history of secrets he did not want disturbed. To do so could open family members to legal troubles.

My position as secretary to Chinese gang came to abrupt end when my father and grandfather called me into private meeting and informed me that I needed to be done with it.

I quit gang and turned my attention to somethings that were more fun-driving fast cars and chasing girls.

Chapter Nine
 презаря

My high school years

My high school years were spent in Tranquerah English School. This school was named for explorers who founded Malacca, Malaysia. Just as USA honors Christopher Columbus, you remember Columbus, right? Malacca honors Tranquerah. Tranquerah Mosque in Malacca was first built in 1728 after Dutch relaxed rule on freedom of worship of non-Protestant faith. Design of Tranquerah Mosque reflects elements of Sumatran architecture demonstrating that Islam has been in Malaysia for 600 hundred years.

As name implies, Tranquerah English School was operated by British government. I was taught both to read and write English at this school. Uniforms required for this school included a white shirt-again, must be pressed, with necktie and kaiki colored, long brown pants. Necktie burned, hot in tropical temperatures. Long pants also hot.

We not only studied English, but all typical subjects such as history, mathematics, music, art, handwriting and the sciences such as biology, physics, astronomy and others. We also were led in physical exercises each day. We were taken outside to grassy, green fields surrounded by lush tropical growth of palm trees, tall Bougainvillea bushes dripping with blood-red or white, yellow, purple or pink blooms. Blooms so large and heavy that the entire bushes were tilted over to the ground like a long-necked giraffe stooping to drink water from a cool river. Green vines wound up and around on garden fences in the ever-seeking effort to touch the sunshine.

We were told to line up in a straight line and were led in jumping jacks and other exercises of this nature. Fragrances of flowers-roses or lotus were strong and aromatic, pulled into our lungs as we breathed deeply due to increase of our heart rates. Who would not want to see and to smell these things?

Our classes also included shop-wood shop in which we learned how to use lumber, how to make things-tables, chairs. How to use metal tubing. We probably made things like baskets and I know we made paper lanterns.

There is long-standing tradition, a contest, in this school to select most well-made paper lantern each year. It's a big deal. I never won.

Girls were taught how to sew and make preparations to be good wife. Girls did fan dances and dances with colorful ribbons. School was full of lots of interesting activities both to fill our minds and to keep us busy. If there was a baking contest, my sister Margaret always won. Even today Margaret's recipe for pineapple tarts is popular. She has a long waiting list for customers who order this tasty treat.

Throughout the years I have had numerous friends. My godbrother, Albert Tan, is a schoolmate and close pal. Friends who stuck with me through thick and thin are Steven Lim, William and Sunny Chua. We spent many happy times talking about cars and going to parties. We all loved fast cars and pretty girls. Andy Goh and Yap Tuck Meng` are also close friends to me. Siah Chin Huat, my uncle George's brother-in-law, is life-long pal. Distance cousins, Cass Lim and Donn Tann from Penang are members of the Lim Clan, too.

**Richard Ong Lin Chuen,
Phillip's best friend from his childhood
in Malaysia.**

Chapter Ten

Womanizing Parties

Throughout my childhood and even after I became young adult, my grandfather's family continued to increase in size. He had sixteen grandchildren. When we boys became teenagers we became another big part of one of our grandfather's favorite things womanizing parties.

Grandfather loved hosting womanizing parties for family members and for friends and local businessmen. For these parties he rented great banquet halls or private rooms in expensive restaurants. He gathered male members of his family around him as if we were knights at King Arthur's Court. Grandfather spared no expense at his parties. He ordered finest in meats, soups, vegetables, fruits, sweets, whiskey and women.

Grandfather was womanizer, this is true. You must understand moral code of the time. Grandfather was of Chinese ancestry. He was Confucius-style Buddhist. His wives were Malaysians. They were Muslims. The Muslims at this time were very different from what we hear about today. They were not Sunni. They had more the "live and let live" philsophy. Grandfather practiced his religion and they practiced theirs. There were no dispute. His children were raised in his religion.

Grandfather had wives and mistresses. This was the custom. He had enough money to support as many women and families as he wanted. He loved women and he loved womanizing.

The wives and mistresses were not jealous because their needs were met. If they were jealous or if their hearts were hurt, they kept thoughts private. To complain would cause unhappiness and might jeopardize their position and status within community. Men had access to wealth and, therefore, controlled lives of women. Woman's best defense against poverty was to produce one child or even more for wealthy man. Having child was like having insurance policy. Smart woman know, you can marry more money in fifteen minutes than can work for in lifetime.

On womanizing occasions when grandfather hosted lavish parties, he paid for services of numerous, beautiful women-cabaret women. I suppose nowadays you would call these women escorts or maybe even prostitutes. Cabaret women were a big part of our culture.

Women at womanizing parties painted faces with powder that smelled so good. Used colorful makeup and heavy eye shadow. Dressed in low cut, tight dresses or shorts, dripping in sparkling jewelry, being sure to flash breasts at us. Grandfather had thing for breasts. Don't all men love this?

Women smelled like roses or lotus flowers. I only needed to get whiff of these fragrances to feel myself stirring with passion. Even today, if I smell aromas similar to these, I can feel myself stirring with passion at memories of festive, womanizing parties.

I vividly remember one particular party thrown by my grandfather that could have ended in disaster. For this particular party, possibly twelve to twenty male members of our family and friends of my grandfather were invited. Myself, my brothers, my cousins, one uncle and friends I already spoke about were present.

Plenty of sexy cabaret women present to entertain us by dancing, flashing their breasts, singing songs about love and fondling our faces and rubbing muscles in our arms.

We enjoyed looking at beautiful sexy girls; lusting after them and imagining scenarios of having sex with them. We were getting drunk from whiskey and dizzy from fragrances of roses and lotus flowers while viewing plump breasts and slender legs of entertainers. Women sang and wiggle breasts-wow Who not be happy?

Late into evening, when most were tipsy from booze, one of cabaret ladies began to play game with us by hopping from lap of one young man to lap of next young man, daring us to catch her before she fell to floor. Women were getting drunk, too. We reached for her daring to rub her legs or breasts. It was great fun. We were laughing and touching playful woman.

She wiggled her butt at us like drying herself off with thick towel. We laughed; such fun to see her do this. "I'm gonna do the Twist and it goes like this," she sang, mimicking a song from Chubby Checkers, a Rock 'n Roll singer popular at the time. She gyrated her hips back and forth performing the American dance we all knew from listening to songs on the radio.

"Do you want to know which of your grandsons are impotent?" she teased grandfather.

"Yes," he answered. His interest peeked. He gazed into her eyes raising his eyebrows with approval. He looked at our faces to see our reactions to her question. It was important to our grandfather for the Lim name to continue.

"Try them all," said grandfather. Oh boy, the fun had begun.

Young woman giggled. Sitting in our laps giving each turn at groping her legs and breasts. I felt myself growing both excited and nervous as time approached when it would be my turn for her test.

"Not this one," she said with smile and bounced into my cousin's lap. "Not this one, or him, either," she said wiggling her butt and rubbing up against him.

I grew increasingly nervous. For some strange reason, I was having flashbacks from day I was made to stand in front of my class and receive three whacks from ruler.

Suddenly, painted cabaret woman moved from my cousin's lap onto mine. She wrapped arms around my neck and slowly ran long fingernail, painted with bright red fingernail, down my face. She looked into my eyes boldly touching excitement in my pants. "Not this one," she said kissing me full on my lips.

Everyone at table laughed and my cousin punched my arm. "Good for you, huh?" he said. He took drink of whiskey and grabbed at woman who was lingering in my lap. I remember that I laughed and drank some whiskey, too.

I raised myself unsteadily to my feet, folded hands in front of self and bowed. My family clapped and make crude jokes about my excitement.

I was glad cabaret girl with red fingernails decided that I was not going to be impotent, but more importantly, I was glad I was not shamed in front of family. This would have been disgrace I could have never lived down. I didn't want to be impotent. I didn't want to be perpetual brunt of jokes.

Secretly in my mind, I didn't want to miss out on being able to father children because grandfather not be happy. Passing down his heritage and keeping Lim Dynasty alive meant everything to him. I wanted more than anything in this world to please men in my family.

By making great successes of their lives, Lim Keng and Lim Wah Mooi and Richard Lim Cheng Ann set high bar for men in our family. I knew I had to reach for top. Hill would be hard to climb. I did not know at that time, however, how I would do it. I did know, thanks to the cabaret girl with fingernails painted red and with fragrance of roses, that I was not going to be impotent. She was correct; I was not.

Red Square - Fountain and Clock Tower
Photo by Phillip Lim

Chapter Eleven

My godfather, the Honorable R R Chelvrajah, speaks…

In USA you have this word "godfather." It has been made popular through the movies and television. Marlon Brando, he play godfather. Did it very well. James Gandolfini, he also play godfather in The Sopranos on HBO. Did it very well. Both gangsters. Very violent. Running crime family and such as that.

In Malaysia, there is position of godfather. This is position of responsibility, not like USA movies and television, not for doing bad things.

At my birth, a man was named as my godfather. He is the Honorable R R Chelvrajah. Mr. Chelvrajah was selected as my godfather because he was best friend to my grandfather.

He took the appointment very seriously. He did a good job as my mentor. He watched me all my life in important events. He right there to keep up with my advancements.

He wants to hear about my successes. He is happy when I do well. He is happy when all of Lim family do well. He troubled when see me troubled, too.

I hold him in esteem and in highest place of honor in my life. I turn to him and seek his opinions and always follow them, now that I am of mature age.

Mr. R.R. Chelvarajah was elected as President of the Malaysian Bar in 1991 and is a senior member of the Malacca Bar. He is one of many from Indian background who rose to fame in Malaysia.

According to facts from The Malaysian Bar web site, "The Malaysian Bar is a creature of statute established under the Advocates and Solicitors' Ordinance 1947 which ordinance was subsequently repealed by the Legal Profession Act 1976. It is an independent Bar whose aim is to uphold the rule of law and the cause of justice and protect the interest of the legal profession as well as that of the public of Malaysia.

The legal profession in Malaysia is a fused one with a membership of approximately 12,000 members and its membership is increasing by 10 -15% annually. Each advocate and solicitor is automatically a member of the Malaysian Bar so long as he/she holds a valid Practicing Certificate.

The Bar Council comprises thirty six (36) members who are elected annually to manage the affairs and execute the functions of the Malaysian Bar. The Council consists of the President, the Vice-President, the immediate past President, the Chairman of each of the Eleven (11) State Bar Committees, one (1) member elected by each of the eleven (11) State Bars to be its representative to the Bar Council and twelve (12) members elected from throughout Peninsular Malaysia by way of postal ballot.

The Office Bearers, namely President, Vice-President, Secretary and Treasurer are elected annually by the Bar Council at its first meeting which is traditionally held immediately after the Annual General Meeting (AGM) of the Malaysian Bar. They are full time practitioners and their honorary appointments are subject to re-election every year. In any event save for the post of the Treasurer which is not provided for in the Act, the Office Bearers cannot hold office for more than two (2) consecutive years.

The Bar Council takes office at the conclusion of the Annual General Meeting and concludes at the AGM of the following year. The members serve on a part-time voluntary basis as the Legal Profession Act prohibits payment of fees or remuneration."

Interview With Mr. Chelvarajah: (January 4, 2013 - Melaka, Malaysia: SKPYE to Knoxville, Tennessee: 9:30 a.m. Eastern Pacific Time Zone)

What can you tell me about the Lim family?

I have known Phillip's grandfather, Lim Wah Mooi, since I was a child. When I was a young boy, seven years old in school, we were neighbors. We could look at each other as we were living in houses across the street. He was a happy man. Forthright and open in his opinions and approach. He had a great reputation in the community-a very popular man.

The Asian way is not to discuss personal finances out in the street. Not to flaunt riches or tell of these things. Keep business personal within the family. However, the way a person went about shows if he is a rich person. Lim Wah Mooi moved in social circles, dressed very well, with the finest clothing, also entertaining many people, providing for them. His position with wealth would be apparent. It was obvious.

He often went to Tea Dances. He was dressed very well--in finery. This sort of person could afford these things. These Tea Dances no longer exist, but were prevalent at the time and Lim Wah Mooi was always involved. He was a stalwart in the community in all areas of the culture.

What can you tell me about Phillip as a young man?

Okay, well, as a young boy, I knew him from the day he was born. He was very easy to know. He was not withdrawn. He was very active. He was going about in the community involved in many things. He had a very protective, easy life. He was always very talkative; very active. He always liked to talk about many topics.

Their heritage was hard work and making opportunities. The family members are charitable, good citizens. One of the Lim uncles was part of a group of businessmen who donated an empty plot of land for the Cheng Hoon Teng Temple. It is estimated the land was valued at two million dollars in those days. In today's dollars, the value would be well over ten million, maybe even higher. Land can not be replaced.

Even as a young man, Phillip was always had plans of moving his business into the future. He has had dreams. We talk many times about his plans. He keeps these things on his attention. He now owns a restaurant in America and is planning to open the next one.

He dreams of having a chain of restaurants like Kentucky Fried Chicken or things of this sort.

Phillip is my godson. I first laid eyes on him on the date of his birth. He was a fine looking fellow and continues to be one. When he was 16 and just received his driver's license, he would drive me to my appointments. On these car rides, we had many discussions about these plans. Even at this age, he was planning these things. I was impressed with his abilities as a youngster of 16. I am glad to see his success both with wife and family and business.

He has always been special to me. I am happy to hear his voice on the phone calling me. It will be a pleasant call. He has found happiness with Louise and his children are doing well. He is a grandfather with the birth of Hayden. This is good news.

What makes Malaysia special?

It is a land of opportunity. It is going through a phase like America went through many years ago. We have the Straits of Melaka, one of the busiest waterways in the world. Our country is exploding in business. We have a great environment for business. We have all that one island can offer. We need middle class Americans to immigrant. It would be good for them. Rich Americans come here and build factories. I would like to see the middle class discover our land. We are very influenced by the British. In many ways our education and culture have experienced losses. We will never go back to days and times
when things were more relaxed.

Do you have more comments?

Yes, I will say that my godson, Phillip, is special, truly special. I look forward to reading his book. It is good thing to do this, to write a book. I will say it will contain lively information.

Phillip was the child who enjoyed life more than most. He was the partygoer. He had the abilities to organize and make grand events. People enjoyed his plans; he was successful in this way. There came a time when he had to set aside the partying lifestyle, to grow up, to move into maturity. I am happy to see that he has done this.

He has made much success in the USA. He came from good roots; good training. He was given the upbringing to be hard working and healthy and happy.

Phillip seems to be the person in the family who relates to story of his great-grandfather. He continues to be inspired; this is good. He continues to bring this story forth. He keeps the spirit alive by his memories. In many ways, he is the selected one, the chosen one, the one in the family to record the reason for his family to progress.

The godchild can bring good luck to the godfather. This is true for me. It has been a rewarding experience to have Phillip in my life. He is like a son to me. I feel his respect and his love. To be highly elevated is a good thing. We are highly elevated one to another.

When my phone rings and it is Phillip calling from America, I know it will be a pleasant thing to hear his voice-always glad to hear from him.

Chapter Twelve

College Years in Australia

When it came time for my higher education, my grandfather and father decided that Australia would be a grand place for me to go. Sending their children abroad to attend college is seen as a step towards upward mobility for the upper classes in Malaysia. My family chose Australia. Other family members have gone there as well.

Proper arrangements were made for me to attend Preston College of TAFE in Melbourne, Australia. My uncle, Henry Lim Cheng Hee, who is only one year younger than I, was sent to this college for his training, too.

Henry Lim Cheng Hee and I are two young men, handsome, healthy, excited about life and ready to begin a new chapter-out of our parents' homes and into a new world. We boarded an airplane and the jet propelled us upward into the sky. I think, wow, we are off to a new adventure.

Man, those years are a blur.

I not lie about my past. I party a lot. I gamble. Drink booze. I am back to my womanizing ways. Perhaps I never left them.

Melbourne, Australia was a world of differences for myself from Asia having Asian ways. People there speak English, but not like anything we had heard. They say, "Gud daaa," which means "Good day." Also, "Mate and Shelia," that's stands for man and woman. "Come over, we'll put a shrimp on the barbee," is another phrase we heard a lot.

We soon were used to seeing kangaroos jumping everywhere. Do you know these animals are dangerous? A mid-sized kangaroo can kill a man. They are that strong. We were told, "If you see a kangaroo and you are alone, run."

Man, oh, man, Australian women are beautiful. So many pretty women from many places and ethnic backgrounds were in our college. Woman of all sizes, shapes, races and colors, too. White, brown, black, yellow and a color we had never seen-very dark, very black, a people called Aborigines.

The Aborigines, we learned, are indigenous to Australia, they are the original Australians. History tells us they got the same kind of deal the Native Americans got in the USA. Once white people immigrated to their country, they were shoved aside.

Once you have seen an Aborigine, you will always know how to identify them. They are that different from other black people. There is a special shape, a special tone to their skin; definite differences. Abos, as Aussie's call them, are highly creative and ingenious.

The Aborigines are very spiritual and understand things about the spiritual world that we do not. They also know how to live. How to survive in the harsh desert climates or the Outback-another Australian word.

We enjoyed watching Aborigines throw the boom-a-rang. Wow, are they ever good at it!

This was the first time we had ever heard the music made with the didjeridu. Have you seen this thing called a didjeridu? It is made from very long pole and looks like giant peashooter. It makes sound like wobbling, popping horn. In my opinion, the sad moan of didjeridu is caused from spirits of dead ancestors of the Aborigines. Sad because their county was stolen from them.

Another big part of living in Australia is water sports. Oh Lordy, do they ever have lots of water. After all, entire continent is an island. We had many opportunities to go fishing, boating, and skiing in deep blue waters. The way we ride across waters in fast speedboats exactly the way we go through life at this time-always on high speed with motors revved up to top. We spent most weekends on shimmering beaches watching pretty girls in skimpy bathing suits parading by and giggling at us.

Such beautiful and wild land provided us with more of an education that what we were receiving from textbooks in our college classes. During college years, I partied, I had fun, I drank beer, played cards, gambled and chased women and enjoyed myself. I studied enough to pass my classes, but did not use my abilities.

While in Australia, some guys I knew and I became interested in Ouja boards. The Ouja board (pronounced "WEE-ja") is also called a spirit board or talking board.

Back in those days, we made our own boards. A Ouja board is nothing more than a flat board marked with the letters of the alphabet, the numbers 0-9, the words "yes", "no", "hello", and "goodbye" are usually written along the sides with various symbols and graphics. Another piece of wood is used as a moveable indicator. To operate a Ouja board, someone ask a question, then each person places their fingers on moveable piece and it is moved about board to spell out words that are answer to questions asked of Ouja.

We played around with these boards, asking questions and sometimes, we would get spooked. The Ouja appeared to be alive. Was it watching us?

We also took Ouja boards to grave yards and ask questions. One night, we asked the Ouja board a question and each guy who had his hands on Ouja board heard an audible answer. A loud word, "Yes," came out of sky from nowhere. We threw Ouja board up in air and ran like hell. We never played around with Ouja boards again.

Ouja is currently registered trademark of Hasbro Inc., which markets and distributes Ouja Board as part of its line of board games.

After graduating from college, I returned to Melaka, ready for work for my grandfather and father. I began to do jobs. I did well, however, I was also a spoiled brat. Liked to party. Liked spending time with cabaret girls, in bars, in dance clubs.

I once had opportunity to travel to Hong Kong. Exciting city; lots to do. Many things to see; many ways to spend money. Like I told you before, I went to bank and told banker, I am grandson of Lim Wah Mooi. Great-grandfather, Lim Keng. I told him, "I need money." Banker eagerly give me all the money I want. I borrow $10,000 in cash.

I use the money to go to night clubs like my grandfather. I pay for cabaret parties like my grandfather. I spend on exotic foods, booze and pretty girls. I am womanizer.

Money come due; I have no way to pay. Bank phones grandfather for money, for $10,000. He is surprised. He pays for it; he likes me really well. He not happy with me, however.

From the Official Web Site of Cheng Hoon Teng Temple:
"Cheng Hoon Teng was founded in the 1600s by the Chinese Kapitan Tay Kie Ki alias Tay Hong Yong. During the Portuguese and Dutch eras, Kapitans were appointed chiefs or headmen of the various ethnic communities.

In its early years, besides serving the community's religious needs, the temple also functioned as the official administrative centre and a court of justice for the Kapitans.

Besides Kapitan Tay, other prominent Kapitans included Li Wei King, Chan Lak Kua and Chua Su Cheong. Kapitan Chua was responsible for rebuilding the temple in 1801 while the Kapitans and Teng Choos after him contributed towards the aesthetic and structural additions of the building.

In 1824, the British abolished the Kapitan system and the leader of the Temple, now known as "Teng Choo", assumed some of the Kapitan's responsibilities. Subsequently, a Board of Trustees was formed to look after the temple.

The pioneers included Tun Sir Tan Cheng Lock, who also initiated the Temple's unique incorporation under an act of Parliament {Cheng Hoon Teng Temple Incorporation Ordinance 1949}.

To the locals, the temple is also known as Kebun Datok (Gods' Garden) and "Kwan Yin Teng." Tun Sir Tan Cheng Lock is our relative.

Jasmine and Christian Lim, Gary's daughters

Chapter Thirteen

Coming to America

After situation with $10,000 and bank. My father sat me down and said, "You have lived in Australia. You have graduated from college. You have worked in the family business, but you do not know the value of money. You party too much. You are not serious about your future. You need to learn important lesson-the value of money. Your mother and I are going to send you away. It is time you learned this lesson."

"But, where am I going to go?" I asked them.

They say, "How about America? You like cowboys and Indians."

I say, "Wow, I will enjoy cowboys and Indians." I say, "You sure you want to send me to America? I will have more fun."

I was 29 years old in 1986 when parents arrange for me to apply for work visa to get into the USA. They buy me plane ticket and give $300 dollars cash and credit card, but told to only use in case of emergency. Emergency not dance club or party with cabaret girls.

I land in LA and the agent in Customs ask me, "How much money do you have?" I say, "$300" And officer say, "That is all you have?" He scratch his head.

I was sent to other Customs' officer and he said, "Okay, you are cool and he stamped my visa."

Before this trip, I had met a woman in a restaurant in Kuala Lumpur named Dorothy Bowker from America who was raised in Malaysia. She had friendly eyes. She smiled a lot. She gave me her telephone number. I had kept it, the one telephone number of the woman from America, so I called her from airport in LA.

She said hello, and I said, "This is Phillip from Malaysia. You met me in Kuala Lumpur in a restaurant with Jimmy Lim and Jennifer Chang. I am in LA."

Dorothy said, "I am not in California, I am in Houston."

I could not believe how far from California to Houston? Not help me this night.

I got book with Yellow Pages and I found cheap motel.

I got settled in motel and went out in street looking for cowboys and Indians. But, I did not find them in LA.

I took account of my money. So far in the USA, I buy some food, ride in taxi cab, pay for cheap motel. I am almost out of money and want to fly from LA to Houston. I use credit card and charged plane ticket. It not an emergency, but this went through okay. I am on my way to making a new life in USA and learning value of money.

When I got to Texas, Dorothy let me stay with her for few days.

First day in Houston, I said, "Okay, let's go and look for cowboys? I did not see any in the airport."

She yelped a big laugh at me, "Are you serious?" she asked.

I didn't find any cowboys in Texas. I saw men in cowboy hats, driving pick-up trucks, not riding horses or having guns in holsters buckled around their hips; not real cowboys. Did not see Indians dressed in leather clothes wearing beaded headbands, no bows and arrows, no hatchets.

I remained at Dorothy's place. She was employed and was gone to work most of time.

Soon, sadness crept into my mind, I had these feelings. I was what you would call homesick. So, I called my mother and I asked her to let me come home. She said, "No, you can not do this. You must stay. You have to learn the value of money." I remember that I cry. I am grown man and I cry like child who skinned his knee in bike wreck sitting alone on side of bed.

I had no choice but to stay in house in Houston with woman I had met in Malaysia. Not even my mother would send money; I really in for hard times now. Good thing Dorothy was nice person. She cooked; fed me. Soon, I found out that she was married and her husband, Steve Bowker, was in California. In a few weeks, when Steve came home, he ask, "Who are you in my house? I answered, "I am Phillip, your wife's friend."

He said, "I don't know you. I am afraid there is going to be trouble." He talked to me. We have conversation. I told him about my travels and why I contacted Dorothy. After a while, Steve said, "Okay, I like you. You can stay here a while."

Dorothy and Steve and I became good friends. They helped me to get Social Security card and let me stay with them a while. The Bible has examples of the Good Samaritan-this was Dorothy and Steve. It was my beginning. I had taken first steps in America to learn the value of money, but I did not see cowboys riding on horses chasing Indians while in Houston.

Many years later I did manage to find real Indians. I was living in Tennessee. Found real Indians in Cherokee, North Carolina and made many photos of them. Their ancestors had fled to mountains and hid when President Andrew Jackson ordered Cherokee Nation to be driven from the Eastern United States and taken to Oklahoma and other sites out West. Indians mistreated in USA much like Aborigines mistreated in Australia.

From the Official Web Site of the Cheng Hoon Teng Temple:
"When the Chinese migrated to the Malay Peninsular, they brought along their culture and heritage. Cheng Hoon Teng's architecture reflects the skills of migrant builders and craftsmen from China's southern provinces, mainly Fujian and Guandong.

The building conforms strictly to the principles of feng shui, incorporating the fundamental belief that every aspect of life is closely related to attaining perfect harmony with nature. According to granite tablets, the temple was carefully laid out to ensure a view of the river and high ground on either side."

Phillip's mother, Low Bok Neo, also known as Sua Ah Jee, in front of altar built in her home in Melaka, Malaysia.
Photo by Gary Lim

Chapter Fourteen
ꙅꙅꙅ

Sarah Shicks

As my great-grandfather and grandfather did before me, I have had three marriages. My first wife was not a bad wife, we just never should have married. We were both thrown into a financial position that caused us to seek answers. We thought getting married would solve our problems, but instead, we only made new problems.

In the process of writing this book, my first wife was given an opportunity to tell her side of this story. She agreed to an interview by the author and was informative. She asked that I not print names of her relationships with others. The author and I have honored that request. She was forthright with her memories and I am grateful to her for agreeing to provide much-needed facts.

My first wife is only daughter of Baptist minister. Her name is Sarah Shicks. She was born in 1964. I met her when she was 23. How we met and became involved is a very strange story; very odd. Both were in low points in our lives. Both were young and foolish. Both were in need of help. We fell into a marriage for the wrong reasons. Not a surprise it did not work.

By 1987 I was living in Birmingham, Alabama, working in Asian restaurant doing prep work, washing dishes, serving tables, sweeping. All things that were needed to be done, I did them. It was a hard life, but I learned many things.

Yes, there had been nights during my stay in the USA when I had cried myself to sleep. I made phone calls home to my mother begging for her to speak to my father asking permission to return home. Mother always held firm refusing to allow my crocodile tears to affect her. Previously, crocodile tears had always worked, not at this point, however.

While in America, I had spent much time thinking about my life. I knew that I had something to prove to myself, to my family and to the world. I was age 30 and it was time for me to get serious and to move forward with my dreams.

I knew that I wanted to have a family. I grew up in a loving home with a mother and father who loved each other deeply. I wanted this kind of relationship in my my life. I wanted to get married and have children. Therefore, I began searching for a wife.

In the Asian culture, marriages rarely happen only for love. Marriages are most often arranged by relatives, possibly when the man and woman are quite young. Therefore, I searched for an Asian woman. I was hoping to find someone who would understand this cultural moray. I found none.

One day, quite by chance, I received a call from an Asian friend I knew who was living in Greenville, South Carolina. He had been working at a restaurant there, but it had closed due to lack of business. All employees had lost their jobs. He began to tell me about a girl, a very nice girl, the daughter of a Baptist minister, who was desperately looking for a job. She needed lots of money quickly to solve a problem, but he didn't know what problem. This girl was named Sarah Shicks.

I spoke further with my friend and offered to give the girl a job. I paid her bus fare from South Carolina to Birmingham. She arrived and got off the bus. I was there to greet her. To my delight, she was pretty. I drove her to my apartment and told her she could stay with me until she could make other arrangements. She also went to work as a server at the restaurant.

I liked this young woman she had a sweetness about her. I soon began telling her about my plans and dreams and how I wanted a wife. She had told me that she needed money. She was down on her luck. I turned to my skills as a good salesman. I sold her on the idea of us getting married. We did.

I take full responsibility for the idea of this marriage. When I first talked to Sarah about the idea of getting married, she was quite hesitant. She said during her interview that she thought I was a "nut job." However, she was in a desperate predictiment and needed money. I agreed to help her with her needs.

Looking back on this marriage, I can clearly see that we agreed to be married in order to take something from the other person. I wanted a family and she wanted a provider. Over the years, as I have observed others who have married, this seems to be a reoccurring theme. People marry what they think they are getting and are often surprised at the results.

Soon after our marriage, Sarah told me some news, she had been married before to a guy from Brazil and she had a young son. She wanted to bring her son to the USA from Brazil. I gave her some money; bought a ticket for her to fly to Brazil. She was going to get her son and fly home, but the plan did not work out.

I began asking myself was this marriage a good idea? If woman could hide first marriage and child, what else might she be hiding? Brazil, oh boy, what's up with that?

After that plan fell through, Sarah had more news, she was pregnant. At first, I was in shock. I blamed her. How were we going to afford to have a baby? I made it clear to her that she was going to have to work no matter that she was pregnant.

She did work, even though she had morning sickness. She also tried to be a good wife. She cooked a tasty meal for me each night and did household chores.

I feel shame at this part of the story. She worked on days that I did not work. I had a problem with one of my feet. I had a spur on the bottom of one foot and could not put weight on it. A friend from Malaysia, Henry Goh, came to help Sarah take care of me. It was not a pleasureable time for her to have a man lying around on the couch watching cowboys and Indians on TV while she worked and grew swollen and tired because of pregnancy.

Was I as good of a husband and I should have been? No. Am I proud of myself? No, I am not. All I can offer in my defense is that I was young, foolish and selfish. But problems were brewing.

Soon what Americans call "red flags" begin to fly. Red flags are hints and rumors of things not wanted. People began to tell me things. What is she doing when I am not around? I take notice of rumors about Sarah.

Things that seem strange began to me happen. Phone rings, I answer, no one there. This happens many times. Phone rings, she answers, someone there, but she whispers. This is not good.

Sarah is away from home; says she is shopping. Is this true? I am hearing more hints and rumors. Can Sarah be trusted? Is somebody from Brazil going to leap out from behind bushes?

I become a Sherlock Holmes; detective. Ashamed to tell you, I follow her when she does not know about it. What do I find? Bad news. How do I confront a pregnant wife with suspicions of an affair?

During the next few months, even though she was sneaking around, Sarah seemed to enjoy preparing for the child that was going to be born. She was certain that our baby was going to be a girl. She purchased pink booties, dresses, blankets, and bottles. She decorated a room for baby; everything is pink.

I explained clearly the desire of Asian men is to have a son to carry the family's name. She adamantly protested declaring the baby was a girl.

All these preparations going on same time as suspicions and bad news build.

By the time Sarah was seven months pregnant, I discovered that another person had entered into our marriage, an old boyfriend of Sarah's. Can a marriage survive with a love triangle? Probably not.

During the writing of this book, Sarah asked me to not give the name of this person, so I won't. I will only say that she had affair with old boyfriend. I discovered them one day together at motel.

After I caught her having affair at the motel, she told me she was in love with this guy. She left me for the old boyfriend and it broke my heart. She moved to Missouri, leaving me with no wife, no future baby and a deep pain in my mind.

On Christmas Day in 1988, she gave birth to the child. However, the baby was not a girl, it was a boy, my first son, Barry. When I found out about his birth, I was back to Sherlock Holmes' routine doing detective work for several weeks and was successful. All I knew was she was in Missouri, but I found them.

Sarah did not expect that I would do this. However, when I knocked on the door, she did let me inside. I was allowed to hold my son and to make a photo of the two of us together.

That was one of the only times I saw Barry as a baby.

Sarah sued me for a divorce and it was granted. Our case went back and forth in the court system. We both spent a lot of money on lawyers and court fees. She won custody of Barry and I was awarded visitation, however, how was I going to develop a relationship with child in Missouri when I am in Alabama?

During those years, I made a great friend in Birmingham, Alabama, B. C. Lee. He helped me in numerous ways in my life with my children.

Clearly, Sarah Shicks shattered my dream of having a family. Talk about rollercoaster going down, down, down. It almost crashed and burned.

I take full responsibility for not pursuing a better relationship with Barry. We have made attempts to know one another better now that he is grown man.

Sometimes Sarah calls me on occasion on Barry's part asking for money.

Looking back on this marriage, did it have chance of survival? Probably not. Does Sarah have regrets? I know she does. Soldier man she left me for never married her. She left security of my bed for insecurity of his. Was this a good choice? I think not.

How does Sarah describe me? She stills says that I am a "nice guy-a good person."

It is not pleasant to continue to discuss three wives. Baptist minister's daughter cheated on me with old boyfriend. Seven months pregnant with my son when I learned of her affair. I could not forgive her. She did not want my forgiveness at the time.

Losing my first born son with his important position in our family was hurtful blow. One I am not sure we can ever recover.

Another baby boy born in 1988 was soon to enter my life. This child would become my adopted son, Shawn. He brought joy to my empty heart.

Bing Bing, Auntie Nitang, Auntie Beth, Amparo Balili and Louise Balili Lim

**House owned by Lim Keng in Melaka, Malaysia
Phillip's Mother and sister Margaret live here.**

Chapter Fifteen

Malaysian custom regarding first male child

In Chinese and Malaysia customs, first male child is highly valued. This child carries on blood line for father. In temple worship and many traditions of the family, the first son is responsible for taking family's place of importance in celebrations and in worship. When parents die, first son is expected to carry torch at funeral. This expectation is extremely important to family. If person dies and first born son is not in town, family will not conduct funeral until first son arrives.

Traditional funerals are held five days after period of mourning, temple worship, visitations from family members and friends. However, if first son is traveling, all this will be held back until first son arrives.

Carrying the torch is something we think about during Olympics Games. However, in our culture it is very different thing. Much value is placed on this custom. It falls to the first son to carry torch.

Malaysian ways of grieving for and burying our dead are vastly different from American Christian ways. Even American Christian ways vary from Baptist, to Catholic, to Methodist and so on.

A.P. Muthu Kumara Gurukkal, religious advisor to the Malaysian Hindu Sanggam National Council, says: "It is important to grieve for your loved one. If there is no channel for grief, you can go mad. Seriously. Some people say you shouldn't cry at funerals. But if you don't cry and express your sorrow when a loved one dies, it may affect you mentally and emotionally. Even an animal cries when its partner dies."

Sinologist Dr Lai Kuan Fook informs us that, "In Chinese funerals, when the coffin is being sealed or lowered into the grave, people are usually asked to look away, especially children. Why? Some people believe it is bad luck. This is largely superstition. You look away because you don't want to have a lasting impression that will weigh on the minds of those mourning."

Hindus, religion practiced by Indians in Malaysia, cremate their dead because they they believe the body is made up of five elements – earth, water, air, fire and ether

– and the God of Fire transports these elements to their respective sources at death.

Chinese culture in Malaysia at this time was influenced by four belief systems: native Malaysian, Buddhism, Taoism and Confucianism.

Confucianism, for example, doesn't talk about the next life but it places great emphasis on filial piety. When your parents are alive, you serve them well, according to the proper etiquette. When they die, you also worship them accordingly.

So all the rites must be observed properly. Some of these rites are very elaborate. For example, paper money and material possessions are burnt to enable the departed to live comfortably in the afterlife. It makes the bereaved feel better.

Buddhism, on the other hand, believes in the afterlife and so, at funerals, you have a monk who will chant sutras for the soul.

Elements from these belief systems often merge to form a popular folk religion. Sometimes bits of folklore superstitions creep in. Sometimes you see incense by a tree. Some Chinese believe that odd-looking trees have spirits of the departed and so they worship them.

Shawn, Barry and Heather

Chapter Sixteen

Deserie

For Samson you only have to say Delilah and picture forms in your mind of bad wife. For me, the name is Deserie. I hear the name and I feel pain and disappointment. But, only I am responsible. I did it. I brought her into my life. I refused to be wise. I did not heed warnings.

I was at party one night in Birmingham, Alabama when I was introduced to a very young, beautiful girl, Deserie Baker. She was fifteen; I was 30. Not a wise match under best of circumstances. I soon learned that she had a baby boy, Shawn.

Deserie Baker, is cousin to Johnny Cash, the country singer. Yes, that Johnny Cash. That is correct. "I Walk the Line." "Folsom Prison Blues." "Boy Name Sue." You know these songs and more from his career. Married to June Carter. Carter family also singers.

Deserie's mother is Rita Cash, Johnny's first cousin. Rita is the daughter of Ivan Cash, now deceased. There were nine children in Rita's family. Many problems in this big family. It will take many words to tell of the story of marriage to Deserie.

In Tennessee I learned a statement to describe my situation with Deserie, "Out of frying pan, but into fire."

Looking back at the situation, I know it was Shawn that stole my heart. I fell for this cute baby boy. He was everything I had just lost. When he smiled at me and raised his arms in the air for me to hold him, I was a goner. I wanted to be his dad.

As we were writing this book, we gave Deserie opportunity to please tell her side of story. She refused.

Although Deserie did speak to the writer about the break-up of our marriage, she stated that she would bring a lawsuit for slander and libel if we published this book.

Over the course of many years, Deserie and I have faced many court battles. She won a few, only to lose what really counted in the end, custody of the children.

This book would need to be two thousand pages long to tell of trouble with Deserie.

I will guard my words carefully concerning her, because she is the mother to my daughters and adopted son. They love their mother and I want them to have a relationship with her now that they are grown and it is safe for them to be around her. What I have to say about Deserie can be proven through court documents or with interviews with her relatives. I have right to my own opinion, too.

After reading my opinions of Deserie, the readers will be ultimate judge of her character. What are my opinions of the Cash family? Not good. I will say that Rita Cash was not a horrible mother-in-law. She wanted best for daughter and grandchildren. Even though she had her own struggles, Rita put herself through nursing school. She worked in healthcare until retirement. She tried to do right in her life.

For the others in Cash family, I will ask you, What do you think of people who get thrown in jail for drug and alcohol crimes and who call you asking for money to bail them out of jail? What kind of people borrow money agreeing to repay, but never remember to send cash? No cash from Cash family, this is true.

Do you have esteem for people who steal your car to drive to buy drugs? I think not. Myself not only person family members turn to for money for rent, to buy shoes for children, to bail them out of jail. Also beg these things from Johnny Cash; he pay. He give them money. He help them out. Forgive next joke, but he Cash Cow.

One bright spot in Cash family, however. This is June Carter Cash. She is angel. So sweet and kind.

Remember song from Waylon Jennings, "Good-hearted woman in love with a good timing man?" This is June Carter. "His good timing ways she does not understand."

Why did she ever get hooked up with this family? June gave us answer with song she wrote, "Burning Ring of Fire." She say she "Burn, burn, burn." She knew she was in with drug user, but she fall for him. June Carter had her pick of men. She could have Elvis or James Dean. She fell for John Cash. Who can explain love?

Johnny and June Cash often helped relatives. Their relatives were very proud of them.

Johnny came up, as they say, "dirt poor." He rose to highest level in music industry. He did share his wealth with them.

Deserie's mother connected to Johnny; this is true. Johnny knew Deserie married to me.

When contacted by phone, Rita Cash was pleasant. She agreed to give this quote and permission to use it in this book: "Phillip Lim is a wonderful father to my grandchildren. He has stood by those kids. I have a lot of respect for Phillip. He adopted Shawn when he was a month old. He has never shown any difference to Shawn than to the girls who are his biological children."

Rita signed the consent papers in order for Deserie to marry me since Deserie was only 15 years old at the time.

During an interview over the phone, Rita said, "I gave my permission for her to get married. I guess it makes me look bad, but Phillip offered to give Deserie and the baby (Shawn) a steady home, and he did. I think it was the best thing for my daughter and her child at the time."

Perhaps the marriage began for the wrong reasons, but it lasted for seven years. Deserie made me happy by giving me three wonderful children and unhappy by taking the children away and dragging me into court.

Was it a thousand times we went to court? Maybe not, but it felt like it.

Heather,
Barry and Shawn

Shawn, Heidi and Heather
PC Lee from Malaysia helped babysit the children and I babysat his kids.

Gejah Berang High School, Melaka, Malaysia

Chapter Seventeen

Melaka no place for Deserie

This is where rollercoaster ride of my life travels down to one of the lowest points at very fast speed. Look out! A wreck is about to happen.

While married to Deserie, opportunity knocked in Melaka for me to return home and operate several restaurants. Deserie agreed to go, I think out of curiosity and intrigue. I had described my homeland to her as sort of Garden of Eden. She was eager to see for herself and experience the Asian way of living. Why not go? It was an exciting adventure for her to visit this strange and unique land.

We moved to Melaka to live in the house where I was raised. I became manager of three restaurants: Dragon Bowl, Best Western Bistro and Hong Tong Thai.

Deserie worked in restaurant as hostess; she was big hit. Customers loved the way she talked with her Southern drawl. Customers grin and clap when she say, "Howdy," or "Nice to meet ya," or "Ya'll doing okay?" The thing customers like to hear her say best was, "Ya'll come back now, ya hear."

Deserie was pretty in those years. She has black hair, brown eyes and creamy skin. She can be a charmer; is friendly-all qualities that do well in restaurant setting.

My mother, sisters, aunties and other relatives baby-sit children while Deserie and I work.

Life was good. We had everything we wanted. Deserie had maid, cook, yard man, and person to drive her around. Money to spend on whatever she wanted. Who would not be happy with deal such as this one? Deserie, that is who.

Day after day Deserie begins to tell me she not happy; she's homesick. She misses her family. She misses USA. She tells me this same thing many times.

Finally, I agree to buy her plane ticket. She can visit USA. This will be cure for homesickness. I am certain.

Deserie travel to USA. Children remain in Melaka. She no call for several weeks. I wonder what is going on? Weeks turn into months and months turn into a year.

She leave children with me in Melaka. She have little contact with me. I assume she never coming back. She deserted her children.

Finally, she call. I pick up the phone. She say she misses the children. She is returning to Melaka She says for me to send money for plane fare. I do. She returned. So happy to see children; children happy to see their mother. My family might be whole again, I think.

Oh, to remember what happens next painful for me. To relive such days and time, almost too much to bear. A day soon after Deserie returns begins as a normal one. We go about our routines. Getting ready for work; getting children ready for their day, too.

I go to work. Leave Deserie and children at home. She is scheduled to arrive at the restaurant later in the day. This is typical. I saw no red flags on this day. Nothing to tip me off as what was to transpire. But, was I looking? No.

The time came for Deserie to arrive at restaurant, but she not there. Time ticks by, she still not there. I call her; she not answer. I call my mother. Mother says, "No, she has not seen Deserie."

This was not the worst news of that day. Within a few hours, representatives of the United States Embassy arrive and send police to schools to get my children.

Just like that. My family has disappeared. I feel helpless. What can I do? Where can I turn? I feel empty and fearful. I pray for the best.

I am asking myself, what has happened? I find out much later what she has done. Deserie went to the USA Embassy. She wants out of Malaysia. She wants to take the children and return to USA. She arranges for the trip. She invents a sad story; say I a bad man. She even said I had kidnapped the children, but she the one who left them for over a year. People believe her nonsense. They provide plane fare. She flies away to USA taking my joy with her.

My world is on an airplane traveling away from me. How can I survive this pain? I am wondering if I will ever see my children again. Will I ever tuck them into bed? Will I hear them say, "I love you, Daddy?"

There were times in my life when I cried for selfish reasons-to get money, mainly. Now I am crying because my heart is broken. Did you ever have your heart to break? It is possible. I know about it now. The heart breaks and it feels like a kick in the gut; a bad physical pain.

Oh I cry a million tears. I cry and pace the floor. I cry and do not sleep. I cry and will not eat. I cry all the time. I cry so much my mother and father warn me, "You will cry yourself to death."

I try to stop. I truly do try to stop crying, but the tears flow. This is grief. This is what grief feels like.

My body aches. My mind hurts. There are times when I think I can not breathe. More times when my heart feels like a race horse running very fast.

I cannot feel better. I cannot move forward. I have lost my reason for living. I have lost the joy in my heart.

My pillow is wet with tears. My body will not move. I take to the bed. I may as well be paralyzed. I am of no use to anyone.

How did I make it through this time in my life? How can anyone survive a time such as this one?

I was able to live through this pain only by the love shown to me from my family. My mother sitting calmly by my bed speaking softly to my ear. Gently petting my arms. My father standing like sturdy oak tree showing his support. Giving wise counsel. Ready to provide money if that is necessary.

I have a theory concerning time. When you are happy time flies. When you are miserable time ticks by slowly. The passage of time is relative to the situation. See? The time my children were missing and gone to the USA crept by like an old turtle crawling beside a river waiting to die.

House on Heeren Street where Phillip's mother was raised.
Photo by Phillip Lim

Chapter Eighteen

Good news! Reunited with kids.

About two weeks after Deserie and children boarded jet and flew to the USA, a call came from a church in California. I took the call. It was Deserie. She had worrisome tale. After her plane arrived in Los Angeles, the United States government cut her loose. They had no money, no support for her. Told her she was on her own. She phoned her family for help, but no one had any money. By the time she paid for motel room and some food for herself and the children, she found herself penniless. She told me she turned to the church for help.

I felt fear. Were my children even safe?

She requested that I send her $1,500; I refused. I am not going to pay her to remove my children to the USA. I tell her I am on my way to the USA. I will fly to America. I will see my kids. I will feed them and provide for their needs.

Before I board the jet headed for America, I sit with my mother and father to discuss my options. We realize that the children cannot return to Melaka. If I want to live with my children, I must live in America. This means I could lose my businesses in Melaka. My parents tell me, "Go, do what is best for the children."

I cannot wait to board the plane and fly to LA. I cannot wait to hug my kids. But, by the time I get to LA, Deserie and the kids are in Arizona with some of her relatives.

I travel to Arizona and finally get to see Shawn, Heather and Heidi. I am happy to see my children. They run into my arms. Plenty of hugs for Daddy.

Thus began a new road. A road to disaster. A road that included divorce and custody battles. Out of love and respect to my children I will not go into the details. Who wants to put dirty laundry out for world to see? Not me.

Let's just say, the courts were kept busy-full of lawsuits between Deserie and me. Only lawyers gain wealth from these proceedings. Years passed and the battles continued. I spent a small fortune on legal fees and lawyers. However, I finally won the ultimate battle. It was the thing I wanted, custody of the children. A new phase of my life was to begin-the life as a single father, a Mr. Mom. My brother Jimmy nicknamed me Mrs. Doubtfire after character in a movie. He calls me this name because of the way it was around my house raising three kids as a single dad.

The kids and I had our daily routines of getting ready for work and school, doing housework and chores, going to church, band and soccer practice, doing homework, going to cheerleading practice and attending ballgames and other functions at their schools. Oh, how about all the supplies and gadgets they needed? Shopping with girls for the fashions of the time. Taking them to movies, watching TV shows they liked and listening to their loud music and arguments.

I am the kind of dad the kids could turn to with their problems. I spent a lot of time listening to them. I encouraged them to tell me what is on their hearts.

I spent a lot of time asking, "Are you hungry?" "Did you remember to brush your teeth?" Yelling at them, "Turn that music down!" "Stop fighting with your sister." All typical daily living in our family during those times.

I did well financially. I was a good provider. The kids had what they needed. I provided stability and safety. No one was hurting them. They also had the most important thing-my love.

David Posner, Phillip's friend who traveled to China with him.

Chapter Nineteen

God's Messenger

I was single man over nine years. People were always trying to fix me up with another wife. I not ready. I was fearful. I take my time; use more caution. Search for different qualities other than good looks and sexiness.

One day my brother, Arthur, from Malaysia called me and said, "Hey, there is this cute girl in China. A singer; very beautiful. You need to go to China and check her out. She might be good wife for you."

At that time, for last nine years I had worked at West Town Mall for Sears-Roebuck. Was salesman; very good one. Won several awards. It was the year 2000.

For what would be my first trip to China. I didn't want to go by myself. I asked colleague at Sears, pal, David Posner, "Do you want to go with me to China?"

David said he would like to go, but he didn't have money for a trip such as this.

I told him, no problem. My family will pay mine and your expenses. He said that he would like to go, then, under these conditions. We made our flight reservations and time soon came to travel.

I was strong Buddhist from Malaysia, at this point.

Buddhism was religion of my family long time through the generations. I saw no reason to change.

I do not enjoy talking about ex-wives, but must do so to tell story of trip to China.

Like I said, my second wife was cousin to Johnny Cash. For the trip to China, you must know that there was bad divorce between me and cousin of Johnny Cash. Bad things about my children. Bad things in court.

When the kids tell the judge they want to live with me, I was living in Knoxville, Tennessee. I moved to Knoxville to be near my friends and brothers who had moved to Tennessee by this time. I am their father. I want to be big part of their lives.

Because I thought it was good for them, I let my children go to Temple Baptist Church, even though I was strong Buddhist. They go to church there for six years. Court system said this was good thing said to do. I was glad for this to be this way. I go with them each Sunday; good for family. Baptists at Temple Baptist Church always wanted me to turn from Buddhism to be Christian. I attended church every week for six years, but still not Baptist.

At one point, the church hosted a World Conference about nations. Freedom of religion, or not freedom. Lots of people from foreign countries were speakers. Many stories were told in that conference from countries like Canada, Mexico, Japan, Brazil and so on.

Knoxville is very multi-cultural city due to existence of University of Tennessee. Students enroll from around the world to study there.

For the World Conference, I was asked to speak about my home country, Malaysia. I said, "Yes, I will do this. I will prepare."

On the night just before I speak, lady from Burma turned to me with request. She was supposed to speak last. I was in line for next to last, but she asked me if we would trade order for our speeches and I agreed that we could switch the order of things.

She spoke about her country and how terrible it was concerning freedom of religion. She went to altar of church before me. She was telling her story and she was crying. People in audience were crying. She gave good speech. She did very well.

By the time it was my turn, I was shaking; I had never done speech in front of 1,500 people. That is the number attending that conference. But, when I stood up and arrived at the altar in the church to speak, I did not have fear.

Whatever I felt when I was sitting there I did not feel it while at the altar. Something at the altar calmed me and I had no problem. I did very well. Was not trembling.

So just after I spoke about Malaysia and how I came to America. I did very well- no mistakes, no trembling. Lots of people came into receiving line and told me their opinions. They shook my hand and told me they liked the speech. Some hugged me. Some of the people said, "They saved the best for last"

So, I was pleased to do well with the speech. But, I was still Buddhist. Something did begin to stir in my heart. What had affected me at the altar? What force took the fear away? What gave me inner strength and peace?

So, afterwards, I single man for nine years. My brother thinks I need wife. He phone me and has idea about girl he wants me to meet. Girl lives in Shenyang, China.

Idea of traveling to China becomes real to me. I had never been there. After all the years of hearing about great-grandfather's escape from brutal government in China, this was my first time to see this country for myself. I was excited. I made decision. Yes, I will go. I will gaze at same stars Lim Keng saw in the sky. I will breathe same air. Walk on same earth he touched. It is my destiny to do these things.

Date arrived and my pal, David, and I left Knoxville on small airplane. Little plane had pilot and two wings and that was about it. It was like child's toy. Motor could barely go putt, putt. We landed in Detroit and changed planes. Gladly. The next airplane was 747.

Large, able to hold many passengers for long flight to Asia. The flight to China was nearly full, however, in row where I was sitting, empty seats. This made me happy, with empty seat next to me, on long flight to China it would be good to be able to stretch my legs.

We were on big plane and the flight attendant said, "We are going to shut the door and we are going to fly."

Just about at this time, the engine was giving that sound engines give when about to push plane forward, but, captain came on and said, "We have delay."

Engines stopped purring; all quiet and delay lasted 10 to 15 minutes. Plane door open and we took on more passengers.

Next, people came and sat beside me. I was very angry. I wanted to have room to stretch. But, because of delay, more passengers now on plane. Seats next to me now taken. I put head down; closed eyes, didn't want to talk to anyone. I'm pouting.

Plane taxied to runway and lifted into sky. We flew out of Detroit. I remained quiet and withdrawn for two hours; still angry.

A gentleman, who became the one sitting next to me, looked at me and began a conversation. He asked, "Are you going to China?"

This made me even more angry and I reacted with smart answer. I wanted to ask, "Are you dumb or what?" But, instead, I said, "This 747 plane is headed to China. Yes, I am going there."

The man began to speak in a pleasant voice. He described his life as one of being a missionary from Louisiana going to China for underground meeting with Christians. Hesaid, "I give you this advice. When in China, do not use the words God or Jesus."

He said he was going for the purpose of speaking about Jesus Christ in China. He was carrying Bibles in his luggage. He also said, after his trip, star football players from the NFL in the states were traveling to China. The NFL players were going to give their testimonies about Jesus Christ.

The minister said this helped out with the underground meetings. The NFL players were good speakers; people responded to their messages and testimonies. He drew me into his world with descriptions of people speaking about their beliefs in Jesus Christ as their Savior.

We flew on. Journey was long. We had pleasant conversation. I cooled down from being angry about not being able to stretch my legs.

The plane landed. David and I got ready to get off the plane. Suddenly, the minister told us he had some good advice. "You need to separate yourselves from me," he explained.

"You will not want Customs' officers to think you are traveling with me. You are not in my group or from my church."

So, we made efforts to separate ourselves from him. We quickly took his e-mail address for future use.

When we were processed at Customs in Beijing, China, the minister was held by the officers. He was separated and we didn't know what was going on. David and I asked, "What's this? What is going on?"

I remembered the minister had said not to use the words God or Jesus when in China. I took this very seriously. I assumed his difficulties were surrounding his position as a Christian minister.

David's bags and my bags were searched in Customs, but we had no difficulties. We saw minister's two bags were taken away to a back room. The minister was held at check-in counter, waiting for his two bags. Both bags were full of Bibles.

Next, a very strange thing happened. One of the bags was returned to the minister. One was taken from him. Both bags were the same; both held Bibles. One was taken; one was returned. We were in Beijing. We flew on to Shenyang, China. Shenyang is in Northern China nearer to Russia than Beijing.

Being in China brought a flood of memories to my mind. Would I walk on the earth in a place also walked on by Lim Keng? Will I touch the same soil? Drink the same water? View the same stars in the sky?

Is the spirit of Keng Lim near? Does part of him remain in China with first wife's bones?

I felt my heart racing as I pondered these thoughts

Lim Keng left this land to escape to freedom. Would he be shocked that I readily agreed to travel there? I think so. Would he be happy to know that myself and his other relatives were free? Yes, I know that he would be glad for this fact.

Remember, our trip is for the purpose of meeting cute girl singer from Philippines, living and working at club in Shenyang. She was supposed to meet our plane, but we arrived and she not there. We waited in airport several hours. She not show up.

Darkness approaches. David and I have conversation. We decide to find hotel. It is nearly midnight. Not difficult to find taxi. Next, taxi driver speaks no English. David speaks no Chinese. I speak enough Chinese to tell taxi driver, hotel, food, restroom--those sorts of things.

Taxi driver drives. He continues to drive. Meter on, taxi going click, click, click--meaning we owe more money, more money, more money.

David says to me, "Places are beginning to look familiar. Are we going in circles?"

This point, I say to driver in broken Chinese, "Stop, taxi. Are you going in circles?"

Driver says he is going in circles. "You have not said where to go."

David and I try to not get angry. I say, "Take us to hotel or motel."

We get there soon. Checking in to hotel and, wow, girl at reception desk very pretty. We like her a lot. But, she speaks no English and my Chinese is not that good. I want to try and date her, but we can not communicate that good.

We get settled in room. We are hungry. Go out onto street. Walk and search for restaurant. We walk three, four, maybe five blocks and see blinking sign. Sign says, "Star Hollywood Nightclub."

I say to David, "Wait a minute, Star Hollywood Nightclub is place where the cute girl singer works. One my brother has sent me here to meet."

We could not believe it. We it in nightclub. Listened to girl singing. We think this is same girl. We wait until girl is finished singing. We walk over to her and say, "Are you friend of Arthur Lim?" She says, "Yes."

We say, "We are here to meet you." We meet each other in this way.

I ask her, "Why didn't you come to airport? We were expecting you."

She said, "The date to meet your plane is tomorrow." She had recorded the wrong date on her calendar. One day off.

We ask girl to visit with us, but she says she has to go home and rest. She has to sleep, but she will meet with us on the next day at 11 a.m., so we return to room and rest.

Exactly at 11 a.m., the girl singer is at our room. She takes us around. Shows us the city. Tell us history of and things such as this. We had great time. Soon, she finished with us and said she had to return home to rest for night of work. We parted company at that point. There was not a love connection.

David and I decided to walk around. To do more touring of the city. We walked and looked. So many people everywhere we went. We walked miles and miles.

We saw large malls; many people. You can not believe the number of people. Something we do not see in USA.

After we had been on the street many hours. It was approximately 3 p.m. in the afternoon. Chinese woman being somewhere between 50 to 60 years old, was walking behind me. It was not comfortable for me. She maybe was following me.

After a while, she whispered in my ear, "God is with you." I felt hairs on back of my neck stand up. It was creeping me out. Her whispering about God was scaring me.

Remember, the minister had said to not use the word God. Was she with the Secret Police of China? Was she setting me up? I was fearful. I did not reply or even look at her.

David and I continued to walk.

The lady whispered again, near my neck, "God is with you."

I ask David, "Did you hear her?"

"Yes," he said. His eyes grow larger. Sweat pop out on my forehead.

David and I decided we needed to stop and look at this woman. We did. She did not speak English. We did not speak enough Chinese to communicate, but we understood her.

She asked to visit us at our hotel the next day. We understood her and agreed. We were puzzled. What is going on that we understood her and she us?

We continued to walk and toured some more. We were fearful. Did we do the correct thing to give the woman our room number? We bought some food. We toured some more and returned to our room. It was not a good night. We were fitful. What was going on
with the woman who whispered, "God is with you?"

At exactly 11 a.m. the next day, the woman knocked on the door. She was accompanied by a younger woman, maybe 20 to 25 years old.

David and I thought maybe this is a mama san, wanting to sell the sexual services of girl.

Was girl prostitute?

Oh boy, our thoughts were way off base. Women were very nice people.

Older Chinese woman walked to telephone in our room and touched while putting finger across her lips. We understood. "Do not answer telephone."

She also whispered. We understood. "Keep voices down."
In the room, David and I sat on the bed. The two women sat on two chairs.

They spoke no English. David spoke no Chinese. I spoke very little Chinese. However, the four of us spoke words and totally understood each other. We communicated. We spoke for over thirty minutes and thoughts and ideas were clear.

The women were speaking to us about God.

Bible scholars tell me there are thirty-five scriptures that refer to the term "speaking in tongues." These verses from the book of Acts 2 (King James Version), most clearly describe what happened to David and myself on this day in China.

1 And when the day of Pentecost was fully come , they were all with one accord in one place. 2 And suddenly there came a sound from heaven as of a rushing mighty wind, and it filled all the house where they were sitting. 3 And there appeared unto them cloven tongues like as of fire, and it sat upon each of them. 4 And they were all filled with the Holy Ghost, and began to speak with other tongues, as the Spirit gave them utterance. 5 And there were dwelling at Jerusalem Jews, devout men, out of every nation under heaven. 6 Now when this was noised abroad, the multitude came together , and were confounded, because that every man heard them speak in his own language. 7 And they were all amazed and marveled , saying one to another , Behold , are not all these which speak Galileans? 8 And how hear we every man in our own tongue, wherein we were born?

Refer to verse 6. "...every man heard them speak in his own language." This is what happened to David and myself on this day in China. It was awesome.

At one point, the Chinese woman told us that she was working with a group of underground Christians. There was that word again, "underground." The same word used by the minister on the plane. What a coincidence?

Soon, woman gave package, small gift to David. "Open when you return to America." He understood.

I asked in jovial way, "Why are you not giving gift to me?"

"You are not Christian," was her answer.

I'm amazed. How did woman know I am Buddhist, not Christian?

At this time, the young woman left the room like she was in big hurry.

The older Chinese woman turned to me and handed me package. Not gift; package. She told me to take this package on journey when I return to USA. It is wanted there.

Suddenly, as if the whole event was foggy dream, the woman was gone.

David and I looked at each other. What is going on with this trip to China? We could not speak the language, however, we communicated with the two women.

We were suddenly very tired, so we rested and had discussion of strange communications.

Next, we take up the idea of returning to the check-in counter of the hotel to make date with pretty receptionist since we believe we have newly found ability to communicate.

However, when we attempt to speak with her as we had spoken with two other women, we do not continue to possess this ability. Check-in counter girl does not understand us and we can not understand her.

David and I looked at each other. Wow! We are really getting spooked.

Next day, we think about how minister on plane gave us his e-mail address. We think woman and minister need to meet since both are working with underground Christians. We walk and find internet café. It is upstairs in building on busy street. We walk up steps and sign on to computer. We type in address and write message to minister about finding woman who works with underground Christians. We tell him about her belief in God and Jesus Christ. We send e-mail and it returns.

David says, "Let me look at the address you copied on the paper?" He did; it was same address.

Next, David say, "Maybe if we remove words about God and Jesus Christ, the e-mail will go through." We did and the e-mail was not returned to us.

Suddenly, we heard police whistle. We began to run. We ran down steps on one side of building. We looked and who was running up steps on other side? Police. They were coming fast.

We were scared out of our minds. We ran fast and ran and ran some more. We stopped when we were huffing and puffing. Could run no more. I said, "Let's grab cab." We did.

David and I were trembling. We were fearful. We are in foreign country. If Chinese throw us in jail, they will not give us even one phone call. We could be in jail for years and no one would know our fate.

I am thinking, "Great-grandfather, Lim Keng, escaped from evil communists, and I may find myself imprisoned by them." Wow, not good thought.

Man, were we afraid. Talk about hands shaking; knees trembling. We were fearful of jail. We were fearful for our lives.

We returned to hotel room and could not rest. Each time door would slam or we hear voices in hallway, we fear it is police coming for us.

David is wondering, "Geez, what have I gotten myself into?" I not blame him.

We regrouped our emotions. Time in Shenyang came to end. We flew back to Beijing and we were so glad.

New problem. It was time in China for celebration of anniversary for Chairman Mao. Many people moving around.

Military parades and more events in streets. Our timing for this trip allowed us to see many communists. Many celebrations.

While in Beijing, we met with friend who had provided us with her phone number. She was from Birmingham, Alabama, USA and living in China with husband who worked there. She was happy to see other Americans and have chance to speak English. She took us on tour of Tiananmen Square and told of much history of famous 1989 protests. Bright spot in strange and fearful journey.

Man, 10 days in China were disaster. We were running for our lives. All to meet cute girl at nightclub and she didn't even like me.

We did have some good days. We did enjoy touring. We were glad we saw the cities and people and history of China.

One huge problem looming for our trip home. Chinese Customs. While going through Customs, I am thinking. Oh boy, they will find package of woman working with underground Christians and I am in big trouble. I do not know what is in package, but how could it be good news for me?

Hands getting sweaty. Knees shaky. Breathing heavy. Trying to remain calm. Keeping head down.

We expect packages to be taken from us. When we go through Customs, one agent inspect David's bags; one agent inspects mine. Agent who inspects David's bags goes through each item. Even looks inside socks. Agent who inspects my bags, does not even open them.

I almost ask agent, "Aren't you going to open my bags?" But, I stop myself just in time. Good time to keep mouth shut.

Return trip was long, but we finally landed in Knoxville, Tennessee. So glad to touch down.

When arrived home, David unwrapped gift, like he was told to do. Gift was candy.

I unwrapped package woman entrusted with me. It was book-Chinese Bible Book. A name and telephone number was embossed on front cover. Man living in New York City. I dialed phone number and explained to man who I was and how I got Chinese Bible Book; how I got his name and number.

"Oh," said man. He was so excited. "We have been waiting for this day," he said. "We have been waiting for your success."

Man in New York explained importance of the Chinese Bible Book.

"Many, many years we have tried to tell people that Bible has been interpreted in Chinese, but no one knew for sure it is being used inside China. This book has never been taken out of China. It can not be mailed out. It can not be handed to anyone. It can not be attached via e-mail. It can not be sent in any way. Chinese leaders say the book does not exist. This copy proves that Chinese Christians do have Bible book to read. Chinese Christians can read Jesus' words; can study about God."

Suddenly, in my heart and mind, I have strong feeling from God. I know I became God's Messenger. I was the one man who was able to bring Chinese Bible Book out of China. What joy came into my heart!

Six and one half years I attended church at Temple Baptist Church.

Members and pastors often spoke to me about becoming Christian, but I am Buddhist. I saw no reason to change.

I live in city in which you see church on every corner. I am Buddhist. This number of church buildings had no affect on me. I saw no reason to change.

I was married to daughter of Baptist minister at one point in my life. He often spoke to me about becoming Christian, but I am Buddhist. I saw no reason to change.

When I learned from man on phone in New York City that I had been chosen to bring Chinese Bible Book out of China, something happened in my heart. I traveled the Pacific Ocean searching for cute girl who was singer, however, I not win affections of girl. I find God. God found me.

I returned to Temple Baptist Church with my story of the 10 days of disastrous trip.

For many years, I had attended International Sunday School Class. James Zanker was our pastor and leader of the class.

At the first opportunity, I spoke to group about all strange things that happened during my trip. I listed the following things:
Delay of plane that just happened to put minister of underground Christians beside me.
Taxi driver driving in circles, but taking to hotel nearest to girl singer from Star Hollywood Nightclub.
Way David and I walked in huge mall after huge mall passing thousands of people, yet, one woman found us.
One woman whispered in my ear, "God is with you."
Meeting young woman in hotel room and speaking in tongues to her and woman who gave us gifts.
Being given the gifts to carry back to Knoxville.
Fiasco with the internet café. Being chased by the police.
Touring Beijing during celebration for Chairman Mao.
Customs' inspector not searching my bags.
Returning to Knoxville happy to arrive in one piece.
Discovering the Chinese Bible Book.
Delivering the book to the man in New York City.
God finding me.
I find God, not in Knoxville, but in China.

Not a single dry eye in class. I no longer Buddhist. I became Christian. I found reason to change.

Chapter Twenty

Eastern ways meet modern technology

One day in 1999 while working my job at Sears, I felt weak and sick. I could not seem to open my eyes. I tried to tough it out, but I got no better. Someone told me to go see a doctor, so I quit being stubborn and made the appointment.

The doctor ran tests and said that I have Hepatitis B. I have liver problems. I was given medication as treatment. Told to rest; take time off from work.

Taking time off from work was hard for me. I am my work, but I knew my body was not responding, so I did what the doctor told me to do.

To my surprise, my kids rallied around me and took care of me. It made me truly proud of them to know that when I needed them the most, they came through for me.

I wrestled with issues with my health for next few years. By 2004 I had gone through several treatments driving to Nashville, Tennessee to see specialists. I eventually went on a leave of absence from Sears remaining at home for many months.

Those years are a blur.

In 2005, my daughter, Heather, decided I should find a wife on the internet. She began searching on web sites and showing photos of women to me. I look at photos and shake my head no, no, no many times. I not interested in a wife. Not after the problems I had with wives.

However, one day she showed me a photo of a beautiful woman who was living in Singapore. The web site said that she was a nurse from the Philippines. Already I was interested; she was pretty. Her bio sounded like she was also a smart woman. Educated; had good upbringing. I became intrigued. Something about this woman was different.

This time when Heather showed me the photo, I shake my head yes. I have to admit, I fell in love with that woman. That smile. That bio of her life as a nurse.

The contact was made and we sent e mails. I requested from her that I would phone her and she agreed. I called her number. She picked up the phone.

We spoke make times from that day forward. We discovered similar upbringings. I found myself growing excited with anticipation of this woman-one so far away from the USA.

After marrying two women with American backgrounds, Asian woman might be better choice for me. Maybe I should find woman who understands Eastern ways.

I pondered: should I get married again?

I vividly remember that I married for the first time out of desperation and fear. I chose a bride who was too young to know what she truly wanted out of life. Because of the failure of that marriage, I lost something of great value-my first born son. My second marriage was a disaster also causing many years spent without my children as well as years of hassles and misery. My second wife had been pretty, but far too young and unprepared for responsibility. I am telling myself, if I take a third wife, I need to be more cautious. I am thinking this woman in Singapore has had an excellent upbringing as did I. She is educated as am I. She is from the East, as am I. Her family and religion are important to her. She has her own independence and knows her own value. Plus, she is a great example for my children.

Maybe I am ready. Maybe I have learned my lessons through my failures. Maybe I know how to recognize red flags or not seeing presence of them.

Louise and her mother, Amparo Balili

Chapter Twenty-one

How Phillip and I met from Louise Balili Lim:

I was born in 1968 in Cebu, Philippines and raised by very strict and wealthy parents. From the time I was a small child, I understood that it was expected of me to work hard, to do my best with my school work and to obey my parents. I am basically a shy and modest person. We are a Catholic family; 100%. I attended St. Catherine Catholic High School. Graduated in 1987.

My parents kept a tight reign over me. They had plans for my life and I followed them. Typically, I did household chores, studied my lessons from school and participated in family events. My parents had busy lives as college professors. They raised me well providing many opportunities for me to learn. We also spent many fun hours with our close family and many friends.

After graduating from high school in 1987, I did what was expected of me, I enrolled im college. With high marks in mathematics and the sciences, counselors pointed me towards the medical field. I entered Southwestern University in Cebu. I received a Bachelor of Science degree in nursing graduating in 1991. Nursing was my mom's field. I followed her into the same career.

My first job was in the Catholic hospital in Cebu. After ten years of working at the Perpetual Succors Hospital, an opportunity to work in Singapore came to me. I took it and traveled there along with two friends. I worked in Singapore from 2003 to 2005. I did well. I liked my job. I was happy. I had a very active social life with friends and associates from the hospital. It was a time of adventure and exploring a different part of the world. Everyone needs to experience Singapore.

As I approached age 34, it bothered my girlfriends that I had never been married. Although I had known several boyfriends, I had not met the person that I knew was right for me. My girlfriends began to talk to me about the internet and how couples were finding each other in this way.

They told me they were going to put a photograph of me, along with a few details, on a web site for Asian couples. I did not object. I found it kind of humorous.

Soon, I was getting e-mails from a variety of men. It was fun, but not a big deal. Frankly, I was not impressed with these guys. I rarely even bothered to answer their e-mails. Some guys sent photos and most were pretty bad.

I had a steady boyfriend I had dated for ten years. I refused to marry him because he had one major flaw-he was overly jealous.

One day in 2005, I got an e-mail from Phillip Lim in the USA-Knoxville, Tennessee. Something about his e-mail stood out to me. Call it fate or an act of God, anyway, something was pulling me towards him.

I wrote a reply to the e-mail. He wrote me back and ask if he could call me. I agreed. We had to set a time for his call that was right for both of us with our busy schedules and the differences in the time zones.

Finally, the correct time came for the phone call from America from Phillip. I immediately liked his voice. He sounded like a kind, gentleman-very busy with big plans for his future. We spoke for a long time and shared our lives. We had a connection right from the start.

My first impressions of Phillip were that he left me breathless, and it seemed like we had known each other for years.

We spoke on the phone, but also spoke using SKYPE. I liked this very much. The first time I saw him using SKYPE was quite dramatic. Before I got a good look at him, I had let doubt creep into my mind. What was I going to do if he wasn't who he said he was? What if he turned out to be an ugly old man? When he came on the computer screen, I let out a sign of relief, he was handsome. Seeing him made my heart beat faster. My fears subsided.

As time went by, he asked me, if things got serious between us, would I move to America? He explained that he could not move to Asia at that time because he had the three minor children, a business and other family members depending on him in the USA. This question began a quandary in my mind. Did I want to live in Knoxville, Tennessee? I was a big city girl. I liked the amenities a big city offered. Would I want to live in a small town like Knoxville?

Phillip sent photos of the three children-Shawn, age 16, Heather, age 11, and Heidi, age 9. I fell for them. They are beautiful children. I would have a ready-made family in the USA. Could I handle three kids?

Soon after Phillip and I began talking on the phone, he asked me if I would meet with his family members who lived in Malaysia. I agreed to meet with them. I became both nervous and excited.

Soon, I met his aunt who lived in Singapore, and his mother and sister, Margaret, who flew from Malaysia to Singapore to meet me. I think there were other relatives there too, like a cousin, or maybe two cousins. We liked each other and got along just fine.

Also, at this time, the position I held in Singapore was coming to an end and I had a choice, sign up for this same job or travel to another job. I heard about a position that was open in Scarborough, England. I decided to take it.

Mrs. Lim had reported news of our successful meeting back to Phillip in the USA. She gave her approval of me. She has always loved me and continues to do so up until this date, and I love her. I admire the job she did of raising her children and doing well.

The next time I spoke to him on the phone I told him that now that I had met his mother, it was time for him to meet my mother and other relatives who live in the Philippines. He agreed that this was necessary.

A few months after I met his relatives and before I began the new job in England, Phillip was able to find the time to travel to Singapore to visit me. We met and flew to the Philippines so he could meet my family. On his trip to Singapore, he brought his two year old niece, Talia, Jimmy's daughter. It is just like Phillip to bring a child along on the journey. Talia's passport needed updating, so Uncle Phillip helped her.

On the day he arrived at the airport in Singapore, I was filled with expectations. His was especially crowded. As each person walked towards me, I felt anticipation only to be momentarily let down. Suddenly, it was as if everyone else in the airport disappeared, I saw Phillip.

I heard a sound like a "yep" leave my lips. The noise coming from me caused me to be embarrassed. Phillip spotted me. He was grinning from ear to ear. My heart skipped a couple of beats. Phillip is even more good looking in person than in photos or on SKYPE. I was not disappointed.

As we spent time together, I found him to be very kind and mannerly. We had a great time traveling and taking care of Talia. I soon learned that he was also hoping that I was not an ugly old woman. We had a good laugh about our fears.

At first at the airport, I was shy. I had brought two friends with me as a support system. His mom was there. We didn't have any privacy. Later that night, Phillip came to my apartment in Singapore and we had a grand time-our first kiss and much more happened. We were so happy to find love.

We flew out of Singapore and traveled to Cebu. Phillip met all my relatives. It was like he was on display. If he had any bad feelings about it, he kept those to himself. He seemed to have a great time. My family gave their total approval of Phillip; they loved him from the beginning.

It was while we were in the Philippines that Phillip showed me a beautiful ring. He asked this question, "Louise, will you marry me?" I was shocked, but very happy. It was a big surprise. He was determined. He knew he wanted me for his wife. I often smile to myself when I remember how he carried that ring all the way from the USA to my doorstep.

Everything was prepared. It was done, I was going to move to America to become Mrs. Phillip Lim. Was I doing the right thing? Only time would tell.

We met in August 2005. I moved to America in June 2006. We were married in August 2006 at Angel's View in Gatlinburg, Tennessee. Phillip had many relatives there. His mom even flew over from Malaysia. My mom, Amparo, Auntie Nitang, and Auntie Beth came from the Philippines, cousin Bing Bing from Canada and my friend, Amy Torres, from Texas were in attendance for my side of the family.

Phillip's kids were in our wedding. Heather was my maid of honor. Heidi was a bridesmaid. David's daughter, Victoria, was a flower girl. Shawn was Phillip's best man. My dress was beautiful. I felt like a princess with my prince Phillip.

So, I did it. I moved to America. Boy oh, was I in for culture shock. My big city ways were not used to the slow ways of country life in a small town in Tennessee. The first time Phillip took me to a mall, I laughed and said, "You mean this is it? This is what you call a mall?"

If I was not ready for Knoxville, Knoxville was ready for me. I put in one application at a hospital and was called for the job that same day. They even wanted me to work on my wedding day. I took the job and have worked that same job since I arrived in this town. I work in orthopedics at Tenova. It used to be called St. Mary's Hospital.

We settled in as man and wife. Has it been all roses and sunshine? No, of course not. We have had struggles with the children. At first they really liked me. After all, it was Heather who had the idea to find a wife for her dad. But, after a while, she did not want to follow rules. She was becoming a rebellious teenager. Home life was not always smooth sailing.

All in all, we had many happy years. Holidays were always exciting. Phillip's children are beautiful inside and out and I developed a deep love for them.

Now that they are older things are better. Both girls are in the health care field. Heidi wants to be a pharmacist. Heather is studying to be a nurse. Phillip says they watched my example. I agree. I think so. I think they did. Shawn has followed his dad into the restaurant business.

Are we lucky? Yes. Get a globe and look at how far it is from Singapore to Knoxville. How would we have ever met without modern technology?

Phillip is a good man. Very kind. A good provider. A caring person. He has a great sense of humor. A good husband. I am a lucky gal.

Amparo Balili, Louise's Mother lives in Cebu, Philippines.

Phillip and Louise Lim on their wedding day.

Chapter Twenty-two

Interviews from family members.

What would a book about my life be like without hearing from my family? Not interesting enough. Therefore, I asked my nearest relatives-my uncle, my brothers, sister, mother, children, mother-in-law, son-in-law, my godfather and wife to discuss their thoughts and memories about me. They have not been coached; they give their own opinions freely. I also get a kick out of reading what they had to say. Here goes.

Notes from interview with George Lim Cheng Hock, son to Lim Wah Mooi and his third wife, who is also Phillip's grandfather.

George is CEO of Lim Keng & Company. Phillip Lim's father, Richard Lim Cheng Ann, was Lim Wah Mooi's son by his first wife. George Lim Cheng Hock is a son by the third wife of Lim Wah Mooi. Lim Keng & Company are owners of an insurance agency and a "bartering" and or "trading" company in which they are exporters and importers of various spices and other products.

George Lim says he is married to Dorene. They have one son and one daughter and one grandchild. George was born in 1956 in Melaka, Malaysia.

Lim Sian Soon was the son of Lim Lian Keng and his first wife who was left in China. Lim Sian Soon was on the journey with his father Lim Keng from Fukien, China in 1899; Soon also survived the trip. Lim Sian Soon was married in Melaka and fathered one son.

Tan Swee Suan Neo was the third wife of Lim Lian Keng. He married her in Melaka, Malaysia some time before 1909. She was a Muslim. She bore him five children; three boys and two girls. All are Lim Soon's half brothers and sisters. Of the three sons, one went into government service; two became bankers, and one became the CEO of Keng's various businesses. The two girls were married and raised children of their own.

The original buildings Lim Keng purchased in Melaka were torn down in order for him to donate land for the purpose of adding to the temple. All written documents from the family were destroyed during the destruction of the latex processing factory.

During his life Lim Lian Keng became involved in the political unrest going on in Melaka between the Malays, the Indians, and the Chinese. He aligned himself with other Chinese immigrants and fought for their independence and against mistreatment. It is said that he may have sold arms and ammunition to the rebels who tried to overthrow the Malays. It is known that he was one of two men in the country who had the certification needed to be an arms dealer at the time.

Phillip's Mother (left) sister, Margaret (right)
Photo by Gary Lim

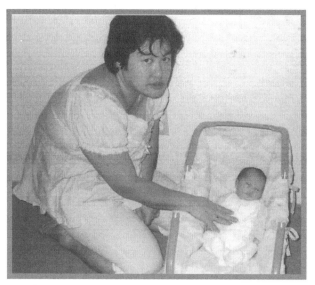

Annie Lim babysitting baby Heidi

Gary Lim and wife, Josephine 2013

Gary Lim-Phillip's Oldest Brother-Speaks from Melaka, Malaysia via SKYPE, January 4, 2013

What are your memories of hearing about great-grandfather Lim Keng?
Lim Keng came from China. He ran away with his Chinese son to Melaka in Malaysia. They were poor. They were hard-working. They were rubber tappers. Through hard work they managed to save money and move up. They bought land our family continues to own.

I had five brothers and two sisters. We live in Lim Keng's house from the day we were born until we finished high school. At this time, we went overseas to live. We scattered; each took different paths.

At the time when we lived in Lim Keng's house, we were very close. We were always together. We had fun. We were close with our parents. We got along. Big family with seven children, many cousins and aunts and uncles, and both grandparents from both sides.

After school we go to the beach. We had fun. We have good memories. Were well cared for. Needs were met.

What do you think you learned from your ancestors?
Yes, I think I learned values of hard work. Of striving to success. Of taking opportunities. Of caring for each other. Yes, my family members are driven to succeed. Yes, this was passed down from them. We inherited some of their traits. Especially to be hard-working. We were surrounded by four grandparents and our parents who were committed to our upbringing. They treated us well. They gave us courage and encouragement. We were often told about ancestors who came in poverty, but who through hard work, became rich.

What kind of person was Phillip as a child?
He happy; always happy. Phillip was the one who was a little bit different in the sense that he was more fun loving. He was the adventurous one. The outgoing one. He spent more money. He didn't save money; he spent it. He has enjoyed his life more than the other siblings, especially in his younger days. He liked parties. At one point Phillip realized he had to not just spend, but plan for his future and begin to save. He always worked hard, but needed to not spend.

Phillip is a fun guy. He always be the fun one in the family. The outgoing one. He a people person. He is making success in USA. We stay in touch. We speak often. He is father and now, grandfather.

Interview with David Lim, youngest brother and family historian, with information about Annie who passed away in 2009.
My twin sisters Margaret and Annie were born in 1958 in order of birth after me in Melaka, Malaysia.

Each of my seven brothers and sisters were born just a year apart except for Jimmy and myself; between us there are two years. Why two years? There was a miscarriage. My Mom lost that child.

Margaret was first twin to be born. Annie came less than ten minutes next. They were not identical twins, but fraternal. Each twin has her own look. I used to say that Margaret is the taller one, and skinnier. Annie was shorter and heavier. They have dark hair and eyes. Creamy skin. Both turned toward being positive, not melancholy. Annie was more like my dad.

Annie passed away in 2009-making her 51. She was a very caring person. She helped the family out a lot. Her favorite thing to do was to bake cookies, cakes and to cook. She never married; Margaret and Annie never married. They lived with my parents, helping my mother out with chores. They stayed close with her. They happy; live happy lives.

They had different personalities. They had their own way of being. Basically, we all get along well. Margaret was closer to my mom; Annie closer to my dad; she named after him.

Margaret has difficulty with speech. Those who speak language of Malaysia can understand her; family can, but others may not. When she was three years old she was playing in grass and a snake came near to her. The snake frightened her; she screamed. Something happened and her speech was affected.

In the Malaysian culture, the women stay at home. This is what is expected of them. Men are supposed to go out and work, bring in the money. Women are to keep the home; care for the children. With many relatives around, there is always much to be done. The twins take care of us really well. They care for parents really well, too.

Interview with Margaret Lim-Phillip's sister, born in 1958-from Melaka, Malaysia via telephone, January 9, 2013.

What are your memories of your childhood?
I grew up well. House was full. We got along. I had both brothers and a sister. My parents instructed me to live well and be happy. They shared with me; taught me many things. I learned sewing; often made Phillip's clothes when he was younger; clothes for other brothers, too.

Do you have a favorite hobby?
Yes, favorite thing is bake, cook. I am known for tarts-pineapple tarts. I sell them. My recipe is famous. Before Chinese New Year's people order these pineapple tarts. I sell all I can make. It is good.

Do you have any other comments?
Yes, it is a good family. We love one another. We have good life. We respect our ancestors; respect our parents. Have good parents; have good home. Well-cared for. It is good.

There was a time our lives were full. Now we see few people. Former days were fun. Memories are good. We have happy life. We miss father; miss Annie; miss others who have gone on to next life. Love our brothers and all wives and children.

Arthur Lim and family

Arthur Lim-Phillip's brother, born in 1959-Speaks From Melaka, Malaysia via SKYPE, January 4, 2013

What are your memories of hearing about great-grandfather, Lim Keng?
What I know is that great-grandfather came from China. I heard stories as young child. Memories fade, but I can say that there is a picture of great-grandfather still in the house he owned in Malaysia. Our family continues to own this house. He was wearing a full suit. He gave the impression as a very successful person. We always know he was successful. He left oppressive government. He was able to escape. He rode to freedom. He became very successful businessman.

We do have good memories of my mother's parents and my father's parents. These are great memories. We enjoyed our childhood. We were well cared for by them. Well provided for. Growing up we were in an atmosphere of love.

In the days of our childhood, things were not so advanced. It was easy living. Not so much in a hurry. Not certain this style will repeat.

We all went to good schools. Not all attend the same school. We had a much, much better kind of education than today. Our education highly influenced by the British.

I'm born in 1959. Our growing up was an eye opener. The country was full of opportunity. From both sides, we drew support, so we were tipped toward the side of having more than most.

Lately we have seen a drastic change in our country due to technology. I am not sure it is for the better. Life may have been more of an ease in days of our childhood. We were blessed. Not sure these times can be replicated.

We lived better than the normal people. We were never poor. We were average and above. Yes, we lived together; we have fun together. Phillip possibly have the most fun of us all. He just that way-fun-loving. Liked to be with people. Liked excitement. We go to parties. Have celebrations. We grew up with these experiences.

By age 17, I joined the Merchant Marines. I was a sailor for two years. It was a good experience for me. Travel. Learn discipline. Make friends. Feel sense of accomplishment.

At one point, I wanted to move to America-to follow Phillip. I actually got the papers drawn up, but I didn't go. I just decided I could make it here. I find my country to be place of opportunity. I can seize the opportunity and do well here, so why change?

I married maybe a bit late; age 30. I have two girls and one son. My children are in their teens. Our home is full of excitement and activities.

There are certain kind of people who look to better themselves. Some are just satisfied to be like they are. We have a trait in our family that we seek to do better. Because of the success we have, we want to even be more successful. Yes, this trait may have come down to us from our ancestors. We saw their examples. Why not be like them? We can see our way to be successful.

What do you think the typical American would need to know about the country of Malaysia?
Well, Malaysia is great place-politically very stable, beautiful, modernized. We have a lot of opportunities. It is a good country to do business. Very much. Many cultures blend together. Must learn how to be accepting of differences-different races, religions, backgrounds, lifestyles.

Yes, things have changed rapidly due to technology. Life is fast paced. Not relaxed like used to be. People hurry to do business. Many opportunities to seize now while available.

Jimmy, wife Ni, son Logan, and daughter Talila

Jimmy Lim, Phillip's younger brother, was born in Malaysia in March 4, 1960. Jimmy Lim speaks from Knoxville, Tennessee:

Everything my brother has told you has happened as he has said. I was in his life to witness from his successes and his mistakes. I saw that he had much difficulty with marrying American wives. After learning from his mistakes, I planned that I would never marry.

I followed my brother to America; he was my sponsor. I wanted to try my hand at living in a country with so much freedom. I arrived in the USA at age 39, joining my brother in Alabama as a lifelong, single man. I was happy in this way. I determined I would live this way-the life of a single man. Life has a way of changing our plans in the most kind of ways.

However, before I left Malaysia, I sought the services of a fortune teller. This is the Asian way, to seek a fortune teller. I was stressed and doubtful about the trip to America. The fortune teller I saw was 87 years old and had been telling fortunes for more than 70 years. She looked at my palm and said, "You are not married, but you will have a life over seas. You must go over seas. You will have a wife, but over the age 40, and it will be over seas."

I kept these things in my mind. I traveled to America. I had no plans to rush into a marriage.

Phillip and I, along with our other brothers and twin sisters, were raised in Asian-style. Over here in America, children learn from the school, not from the home. In Malaysia, we learn from the parents. The parents teach the children the way of life. The law of the family is the law; not the law from the government. Oh, we do follow the law of the land, but the real law is the law of the family. It is the law we must and do follow.

For people who have never traveled to Asia or lived in Asia, there is no way to understand the differences in culture. Asia will blow your mind, baby. There are so many people. Everything is different. Religions are different. The way families expect things from their children is different.

Asian men are different. They are selfish. They rule the home; wives are submissive. Try that in America. Yeah, right.

Over here, if we want to drive around, or do anything, you follow the law, but in my family, if the family says you can drive around, you can, if parents say that you may not, you no drive.

Over there if you want to buy this or that, if parents say, "No," there is no argument; it will not be purchased. There is no whining; no disrespect to parents. No talking back; never.

Asian-style, we look down the road. We look to the future. We consider how each decision affects the next part of our lives. We are very conservative. It is not the Western way to think about actions. It is the Asian way.

Our parents provided for us, however, they made sacrifices for the future of everyone in the family. They were not spenders, but were savers.

My mother refused to buy latest fashions, she would conserve money. Oh, did she have nice clothes? Yes, you bet, but did she spend for expensive things she didn't need? No. Do you know the difference in need and want? This difference is what I am trying to explain. If a child needs shoes because his shoes no longer fit, he get shoes. If a child asks for shoes because the shoes are in style or just sees the shoes and likes them; he not get shoes. Need verses want.

We have a statement that applies very much to what I am describing-the Asian way verses the Western way. Asian way, we say, "We spend a penny; save a dollar." Western way, "Spend a dollar; not even save one penny." How can your society continue with a view such as this?

See, we plan for the future. We will have money in our hands for our children and for our parents when they are old. Will Americans? No, surely not so. If you follow the rule, "Spend a penny; save a dollar," you will not fail. If you continue to spend when you have no money, you are surely going to fail.

Eventually fate took over in my life. I found somebody. Phillip's mistakes made me feel very careful. Phillip's experiences made me even scarier. I saw Phillip step on a land mine. I saw him step out into a huge hole. I would not follow into the same land mine.

His situation with the second wife was bad, very bad. Who would want to follow into the same situation? Not me. I commit myself to stay single. I avoid this land mine.

In America, getting a divorce, just like eating noodles. In Asia way, marriage is important. Different mentality.

Fate stepped in. Met a girl at work. Ni Mariyani is her name. We met while working at the same restaurant. She was an exchange student from Bali. She was working for Dairy Queen. I was working for Mandarin House. I hired her as a hostess. She is much younger than I. We are twenty-three years apart. We liked each other, but I spent a lot of time talking to her. I did not rush. I did not jump on the bus and take a free ride without thinking. I careful not to get involved. We had ups and downs. Mostly, we talked. I was honest with her. I told her, "I am single. I will remain single."

As time went by, I realized, this may be the woman who can change my mind.

I told her my exact feelings about the future. I had no responsibilities. I arrived in America with one bag. I can live anywhere; no one to hold me down. No one to hold me back. When opportunity for good business decision would come my way, I can take it because I have no reason to make a decision except for myself.

She did; she changed my mind. We have same outlook on life as both are from Asia. To hold these same opinions is necessary in a good marriage.

I said to her, "Are you ready for the big step?" She said, "Yes." I told her she was not old enough to have seen the world. This was a concern for me.

One rule I told her. I said, "You may not ask me about my past." She agreed that she would not. I said to her that there is nothing for her to see. If she asked me, I would have to tell the truth and she doesn't want to know it. When she knows my past, if we have an argument, she will bring up my past. I not go for a deal like that.

However, we did get married. I was 43 when we met. I am 44 and have two children. A girl, age 7-Talia; a son, age 3 1/2 Logan. Man, are they a hand full! I love my kids. Do not get me wrong. However, I found out that I am not cut out to be Mr. Mom. I watched American movie, Mrs. Doubtfire. Robin Williams baby-sits children. It looked like so much fun. They love him. He does many activities with them. I am thinking it is no big deal. I keep my own children and after about one hour, I say, "I am not cut out to be Mrs. Doubtfire."

Phillip has babysat with my children. He is a great babysitter. He loves the kids. He can be Mr. Mom or Mrs. Doubtfire. Not me.

Asian attitude is work, work, work. They work too much. Asians are afraid of failure. When they fail, they think it was from not working enough.

Americans like www, work, work, work, but the also want vvv; vacation, vacation, vacation.

Did you hear of the Asian web site? www. S11 S11 workworkwork $$. This is where the Asian mentality is at. Before the www, is HTTP. HTTP stands for Have Time to Party.

Asians have no time to party. We have no http. We only do www. S11 S11; work, work, work, money, money.

We continue to work hard. We will never be out of food. We will have what we need and what family needs. Maybe not wants, but needs.

When Phillip met and married Sarah Shicks, he did not know enough about her to make a decision. All we know is that it did not work. I know much of the problem was the thinking in the Western way. Phillip did not use the old ways. He chose for beauty, for love, maybe for sex, but, not using the old ways. Not looking to the future. At the character of this person. At the family background.

Phillip was in touch with us, but we did not know the specifics. He has always kept in touch. Phillip was very close to our parents. He always calls them; writes to them; shows respect.

The relationship failed for many reasons. She was not a responsible person. Phillip did not know enough about her before he married her. But, how would he find out more? He did not know she had a child. How does a woman keep something this important from a future husband? But, she did. This basis ability of Sarah to refuse to tell all of her story. To refuse to lay all cards on the table. These characteristics are not good. Relationship can only fail. Phillip learns she is in love with her old boyfriend. She wants to be with the other guy. No way to fight against this.

Do you know, you are numbered in USA? You have to live a life in America with three numbers. Do you know your three numbers? No? The three numbers are your credit score.

What is the point of having three numbers? These control the business we can enter into. Even those who do not have money can have a good credit score.

After a while in America, I wanted to buy a house. Owning a home is important; renting may be a waste of money. Paying money for land is a good decision. I discover that three numbers mattered-credit score.

I bought a house. I live there alone as a single man. The girl I marry was surprised that I own a house and live there alone. My credit score was good enough for approval.

Phillip starts a restaurant, the Asia Café. We worked there together to make a success. Next, I started a restaurant for myself, November 8, 2011. I name the place "Go Bananaz," because I serve Malaysian and Mediterranean foods. Are you nuts? Did you go bananas? See?

I build my business by talking to customers one person at a time. I begin small and grow. I am on the upward side, but progress comes with much effort. I call myself a "Mom and Pop" restaurant. It means my customers want to have food, but also hear news, talk to me. I explain ingredients, how we cook, how we make tasty.

Our food is all about mixture of spices. We prepare a specific paste in the old way. Secret to mixture, but we use spices-ginger, lemon grass, garlic, and other roots and herbs. All are common in Malaysia, but not seen in USA. Asians know the real tastes. This is why Asians from around this area drive many miles to our restaurants-to get the tastes.

Asians can sacrifice. We will struggle to do what it takes. We will use the special mixtures of spices. My business not only take my effort, it also has taken 21 pounds from me. I always small, but now, from 128 pounds to 107-weight back to when I was young man. It is stress. I feel it in my weight. I work from 10 a.m. until midnight. I forget to eat. Stress-too much stress.

Phillip, Louise, Victoria, Austin, Donna and David Lim in 2010

Interview with David Lim, born in 1962, youngest child in the family. David speaks January 4, 2013 from Knoxville, Tennessee.

What thoughts do you have about Lim Keng and your other ancestors?
I understand he came from China. He traveled to Malaysia. He was a rubber tapper and work hard and work his way up. He had a business and from there up, it exploded. He got rich.

In those days in China, things were very bad; many were slaves and the government was very bad. He sought a better life. Trip in Sampan bad; only 6 survive journey. Somehow he was able to escape. Brought Lim name out of China.

What memories do you have of your childhood?
Most happy of times. What not to like? Our lives were the best. I remember my dad worked very hard. We grow up affluent; grow up rich.

We all grew up in a large family. We all get along. We are really close in ages. We are a year apart except for Jimmy and myself. Gary is eldest, then Phillip, then the twins, Margaret and Annie. Annie passed away in 2009. Next, is Arthur, then Jimmy and me, David, the youngest, the spoiledest one.

Dad passed away September 22, 2006.

Margaret lives with our mom in house where we grew up-house owned by Lim family.

As a young boy, I loved to visit with my grandparents. I love to look in my grandfather's office. I observe his things. I touch books, papers, ink pens-these things he uses. I view photos of family members on his desk and hanging on the walls. Grandfather keep excellent records of family members. As each child is born, he writes the date, time and name in his book. He had sixteen grandchildren.

One thing he used to have that I enjoyed the most was a book of family records. He kept this book in his safe inside a closet in his office. I often begged him to let me see the record book of family births. He delighted at my interest. He often let me see book. I spent a lot of time reading it. I remember many of the facts.

What was Phillip like as a child?
He was the fun one. He enjoyed life; liked parties; liked people a lot. Phillip was the partygoer. The out-going one; the party one; the out-spoken one. He always like to have people around. He liked to organize parties-this and that. He plans and gets things going-always.

Why did you come to the USA?
Oh Lordy, I came to USA in September 1990. I came to the USA with a sense of adventure. I always liked to travel to see the world. I went to Australia and other places in Malaysia. I always have a good time. I wanted an opportunity to succeed. I also wanted to live near my brothers.

I am making my way as an investor. I am buying properties and making into rental properties. I hope to expand in this way. My father did this; I follow his examples. Things I learned from him.

I help my brother out, too. He is making a new restaurant and I will be helping him with things that have to get done. I will help him with his success. We are a close family in this way.

Why did you remain in the USA?
I got married to Donna since 1993. We have two children, eldest is a boy, Austin

Heng Lim, born 1996 and girl, Victoria Hwei Lim, born 1999. My journey ends in Knoxville, Tennessee. It is a custom for our generations to be named same middle name. My generation is Boon-meaning studious one, I think. I created the name for Austin's generation-Heng; it means lucky. If any of my brothers have sons, their middle names will be Heng.

It comes from an idea from my father who goes to the temple and supplies the idea for this generation. This is important step; it must be done well, with thought.

For Victoria, my daughter, I chose Hwei for her generation. Other girls in the family also have middle name of Hwei. Gary's daughter also named Hwei. Hwei means flower. This is how we keep the generations. How we tell them. The family knows which generation for which you are born into by the middle name. Other brothers' daughters also have this as middle name.

Grandfather Lim Cheng Ann-his middle name was Cheng. My father's was Lim Wah Mooi. Wah is his generation. See? We are third generation from Lim Keng. We are Boon is for our generation. I think it means studious. This name tells our story. It tells our history.

Is your godfather the same as Phillip's?
No, sadly, my godfather passed away by now. In Malaysian culture godfather is like second father. If you need anything or whatever, they embrace you as a son. They have to like you and love you and have a connection with you. A godson can bring luck to the godfather. Getting a godchild is good thing to do. Some go to the temple and ask who would be a good one. A birthday is needed to make this connection. You have to be special to be a godchild.

What details can you tell me about your family?
My family gets along; we always did. Being the youngest, I am absolutely the most spoiled. When my Mom gave birth to me, I think she knew I was the last baby.

As a young child, my parents kept me right beside them. My Mom says I was cute. A good child. Why not be good? I have everything I want. Wherever they go, they take me. Keep me close. I follow my Dad around doing real estate. He was buying and selling. I learned from his skills. His examples. I also follow my brothers around. They carry me on their hips when I a baby. They drag me along holding my hand when I small boy. They care for me in all ways as these. Buy me candy. Poke vegetables in my mouth. Tell me ghost stories and scare me. Laugh at me when I frightened.

My brothers and I share same room; sleep in same beds. They make sure I am covered with favorite blanket. Brothers learn about some things in life before me; they my teachers. They tell me who to stay away from, who to befriend. We always there for each other. We help the other one if they need it. The girls, too. We taught to respect and care for our sisters. Hold girls in reverence. Help them meet their potential. Honor our parents; hold them in esteem. Owe a great deal to them for bringing us up with good values. They work hard, save, for us to do well.

What traits do you think were passed down to you by your ancestors?
The need to be free, not to live in slavery. To work the way up. To be business-minded. To have determination. To be better. To always seek to do better and to find opportunities in business, opportunities to do better to improve. Hope to have luck as did Lim Keng-Keng means luck. There is a responsibility to carry on name of Lim. I do my part. My wife and I have son, Austin. He Lim. He has big shoes to step in. His way also made possible by Lim Keng.

Phillip now a grandfather-Hayden Walden, Heather's son. A proud day in his life to have next generation to be born. Lim name continues. Lim blood still flows on earth in freedom, not in slavery to communism.
Interview with Shawn Lim via phone-January 7, 2013, Jacksonville, Florida

Shawn, Jimmy, Louise, Phillip in front of Asia Cafe

What was it like to grow up with Phillip as your dad?
Good, I had a good childhood. Dad taught us strong values. Not just by talking, but by his example. He was the kind of dad to be there for his kids. He showed us the world. He used the Asian ways-that culture-for our instruction. Dad is not my biological dad, but is the only dad I have ever known. I do not look like his family, but I am proud to carry his name-the name Lim. I was not born Asian, but I was raised Asian. I was always surrounded by dad's relatives and this made me feel their culture.

I have no regrets. If I am ever a dad, I will hope to be as good as my dad. He showed me the ethics of hard work and courage. I hope I have followed his example. I have memories of being a little boy and watching my dad at a restaurant. I was always happy to watch him as he worked. He'd set me on a stool and I'd watch him. He'd tell me to be a good boy, and I would behave.

Do you remember living in Malaysia?
Yes, it is a beautiful country. Their streets are full of people going about in different ways. You may see cars or animals. You see street vendors. You smell food cooking. People know each other. They go to the temple. They have other kinds of cultural things. Ancestors are valued. It opens your mind to other ways of living.

What is your current career?
I am General Manager for a restaurant in Jacksonville, Florida. I run the store-the restaurant. I had training from the time I was a small boy. I saw my dad operating a business. I learned many things from his example. I remember sitting and watching my dad work when I was just two, maybe three years old. I would be good for my dad. That has been the way it was from my earliest time, watching him work. My dad understands my daily problems. If I have something that is bothering me, I can ask him for his advice. He has insights into the business.

Do you have any more comments about your dad or your family?
Yes, I had a good life. It was a good way to grow up. I am happy that Dad married Louise; she is great. She has been good for him. She has been good to us. She treats Dad great. She is an educated lady and a good example. She is a nurse-has been for over twenty years. Dad married her when I was around 16, I think. She took on a lot to take on three kids. But, she did it. We were in their wedding; they made us a part of it. We did have our times of kid fights, but she was patient with us. I guess she thinks we could get loud, too-with music and shouting at each other. But, she made it. She never let it get to her.

Do you have any thoughts about the home invasion?
Yes, I do. It was weird. A scary thing. Not everyone goes through something like that. It just happened so fast. Makes you think about how quick things can change.

I did not have time to think; I reacted.

Dad and I have put it behind us. It took us a long time to heal. We both had a lot of pain. All we can do is move forward. We will not let it keep us from happiness.

I have a good family. Many people who care for me. Dad made sure I know about the ancestors. He made sure I have the values of the Asian ways. I am glad about that. I love my dad a lot, for sure.

Phone interview with Heather Lim Walden-January 6, 2013, Knoxville, Tennessee

What was it like to grow up with Phillip as your dad?
Good. He was a good dad. We basically grew up with him being a single dad. He was the only person there to talk to. Being a girl without having a mom around, it made us closer. He did all the things we needed; got us to school, took us shopping, that sort of thing. If there is a sale, he is right there for it. He loves to save money.

I was raised with my sister, who is three years younger than I, and my brother who is three years older. My sister and I had our differences. We never got along that well. Dad would referee our sister fights. She would get on my nerves. We do not see things the same way. My brother and I got along better. He got along better with my sister, too.

Dad always tried to get us to get along. He told us we were a family and needed to depend on each other. He made a rule if one of us went to a friend's house, the other had to go. This forced us to be with the same people. It got on my nerves, but I see why Dad did this.

Now that we are older, we get along better. We needed to grow up to see things better.

What is your current age and what is your life like now?
I am twenty-one almost twenty-two; married; have one son, Hayden. I work at a hospital as a phlebotomist. I always wanted to work in a hospital setting. I like this setting. I want to be a nurse. I am studying nursing hoping to do well and increase my earnings; my pay.

I worked for a while when I was in high school as a job of a waitress, but I have never been interested in the restaurant world; not like my dad. I did not want to follow his footsteps in this way. I liked working and having my own money to spend.

My husband, Eric, and I began dating when I was thirteen-in 8th grade. We grew up in the same neighborhood; had the same friends; went with the same crowd. Eric is three years older than I am. In 2007, I found out I was pregnant. It was hard to tell my dad, but I had to.

Dad sat me down with Eric and we had a long talk. Dad told us we had to think of the future and not ourselves and not just now. We had to grow up and be responsible. We had to think about the kid.

We took the step to become married and to be parents. It was a neat thing to begin my own little family. Eric and I did well. We didn't have a big church wedding. We got married in a small chapel. I didn't want to do a big thing with me being uncomfortable and pregnant. Eric had a family friend who had this chapel, so that is where we went. It's a nice setting for that sort of thing. Dad helped with the finances as usual. He wanted me to have the best. We kept it simple. I moved out of Dad's house to live with Eric. We got married in September and our son, Hayden, was born in December. Eric works in the construction business; I work in the field of health care. I think-I know, my dad is proud of us. We did the right thing. We did grow up fast with the birth of a child.

What can you tell me about Louise and her marriage to your dad?
I was the one who found Louise on the internet for my dad. I knew that Dad was always lonely. I figured I would go online and help him. I found pictures. I showed them to Dad, but he didn't like a lot of them. When he saw Louise's photo, he got interested.

When Louise first came over to Tennessee, we all got along for a little while, but then, we were not used to having another person around. We did have our conflicts. Yes, I did often say to Louise, "You are not my real mother."

Louise took it pretty good. I was kind of annoying. I was maybe fourteen and still too young to see the value of a person, really.

She heard my sister and I argue and fight. I am sure she often wondered what she had gotten herself into, but she has patience for things like what we did. But, now, I love Louise a lot. We really get along well. She is good to my dad and sweet.

Do you have any comments about your ancestry?
No, I always wanted to not be identified with the Chinese ancestry. I never got in

to it that much. I heard things, but I really didn't listen. I was not concerned. I remember being in Malaysia, but I was so young my memories have mostly faded. I can still remember the way some of the food tasted. I remember seeing iguanas crawling on a bridge we used to walk over, but that is about it. Oh, and it is a long way from Tennessee to there.

Phone interview with Heidi Lim, January 8, Knoxville, Tennessee

What was it like to grow up with Phillip as your dad?
Oh, I do not know. Normal, I guess. I think he was just like any old dad. He did usual things. He was a regular dad, I guess.

Do you have any special memories of your childhood?
No, not that many I guess. I am the baby of the family. I-we did things together-my brother and sister and I. I do remember eating rice a lot. I also learned how to use chop sticks.

Do you have any comments about your Asian ancestry?
No, not really. I do not identify myself in that way. Yes, I am 1/2 from the Asian culture and 1/2 American. I identified more with the American side. I guess that is normal. If I had been raised in Malaysia, I am sure I would be more Asian. I never thought of myself as Asian, only American.

What values did your dad instill in you?
To work hard; do my best. Be sure to graduate from high school. I did graduate from Powell High School. I am in college at Roane State Community College studying prepharmacy. Dad has paid for all my schooling.

Did you ever work in the family business?
Yes, but only briefly. I was never interested in the restaurant business. I never wanted that for a career.

What is your current age and what are your plans for your career?
I am nineteen. The youngest child in our family. I enjoy working in a pharmacy and that is what I have chosen to study; to do with my life. I both work and go to school.

Do you have any more comments you would like to give? Yes, I love Joe and Vondell Stroud, my godparents, who have been great friends to my dad. My friend, Tonya Stroud, is a pharmacist. I am following her footsteps into this career.

Interview with Sua Ah Jee, aka Low Bok Neo, Phillip's Mother, January 9, 2013, Melaka, Malaysia. Mother speaks broken English as Phillip relays questions back and forth using SKYPE.

What was it like to raise seven children in Malaysia?

It was lively; was good. I raised them well. We had a busy home. Many things going on. It was a good life. I did it; I raised them, provided their care. I did the work, and had help It was a good life. I did it; I raised them, provided their care. I did the work, and had help there. An auntie was there to help, and my husband hired people to help. People to cook, to do laundry, to clean. I instructed my children. It was good. We had many people around us. They had each other.

What was Phillip like as a child?

Phillip was a lively and clever boy; a good boy. Very handsome. Very good to do well. He enjoyed people. He loves me a lot and I him.

Do you have other comments?

Yes, I am 74. I was married at age 16. I had a good husband. He treated me good. We had a good family. Big family. We instructed them and raised them good. Each took a different path. The days of having many children in the house, of having many relatives and friends near to us have gone. I miss this. This house was full of liveliness, full of laughter, full of cooking and people, but is now almost empty. The happy memories remain. I have had a good life. Good memories. Good family. Good friends. They treat me well and take care of me.

Gary Lim describes his mother (January 9, 2013) via e-mail:

Our mother came from a very poor family from a rural area called Batang, Melaka. She was born in 1938. Her father and mother, our grandparents, were rubber tappers. She had a brother. They could not afford to raise our mother, hence, when she was 7 years old, her parents gave her up for adoption to a Nyonya Baba family (Chinese culture with Malay influence) from Heeren Street, Melaka.

Families living in this area are mostly wealthy. The family that adopted her included members who were influential in the founding of an independent Malaysia.

Since our mother was an adopted child, she had no education and had to take care of the household chores and look after the other adopted siblings. She also has the name Low Boh Neo.

She was married to our father Lim Cheng Ann at the age of 16 years old. It was an arranged marriage, but it worked out well. Our father was a good husband, an excellent provider. They raised seven children and all were well-provided for and given opportunities and educations.

Mother has had a good life and believes she was very blessed to be a member of theadopted family and to have been married to our father.

Interview with Amparo Gumboc Balili, Louise's mother, from Cebu, Philippines, January 10, 2013 via SKPYE. Mrs. Balili retired ten years ago from her position as Dean of the College of Nursing at Cebu State University in the Philippines. Louise's dad, Luis Balili, passed away in 1996. He was Professor of Engineering at Cebu Institute of Technology in Cebu, Philippines.

What did you think about America when you came to visit Louise and Phillip for their wedding?
Oh, well, I found America to be well-organized. It is a beautiful country. Many wonderful sights. We traveled to the mountains-very pretty. In USA most people travel by cars. Buildings are spread out over long ways. In Philippines we can walk to shops and other places. In USA this is not always possible. Also, in our country we always have warm weather. We have rain, but always sun. In USA there is snow and cold temperatures, even in summer.

What do you think about Phillip as your son-in-law?
When I first heard about Phillip, I was doubtful. He is older than Louise, had been married twice before, had three children, lived in USA, so I was concerned like all mothers would be. However, he traveled to Cebu to meet me, to meet all of Louise's family. This gesture begin to win me over. Louise was telling me that she really liked this guy. She thinks he is the one for her. I soon found him to be quite a guy. I begin to see what she was seeing.

Phillip is a very empathic fellow; very kind; very positive with his outlook on life. He does well. He has brotherly love for many. He is a good son to his parents and a good parent to his children. He speaks well of his children and how he is raising them with values. He is very lively, entertaining, shows manners in his behavior. He treats other people very well. Very talented. A good guy; he has made a great husband.

I now love Phillip very much. He is kind to my daughter; very kind. She loves him a lot. This is pleasing to me as her mother. She is my only child.

Do you have any other comments you want to make?
Yes, I am glad for my daughter that she is happy. I did well with her upbringing. Her father and I taught her well. She has always been a good child; a good girl. She graduated from college and has had various experiences around the world, working in Singapore and England. That she lives in the USA causes me to miss

her; really miss her. Louise she has done well and is happy. Yes, her husband is quite a guy. They have made a good life together.

Interview with Eric Walden, Phillip's son-in-law, January 6, 2013, Knoxville, Tennessee

I have known Phillip since I was in the fifth grade. My parents bought a house that was on a street that backed up to the street where Phillip's house was located. We were neighbors from that point forward. I knew his son, Shawn, mostly. Of course, I met the girls, but hung around with Shawn. Shawn and I were best of friends. We did things together-like pals.

By 2005, I began dating Heather. She was thirteen or fourteen-in 8th grade. I was already in high school-a junior, I think. We dated for two years and had a surprise, Heather got pregnant. She had to tell her dad.

She faced it; she told him. He took it pretty well.

Phillip sat me down and told me it was time for me to be responsible-a kid was coming. I promised to do the right thing by Heather. We got married September 2007.

I am a twin. I have a twin brother, Derrick. We knew Phillip had sisters who are twins. We could also have twins, but we did not. We had one child, a boy. We named him Hayden Sean Walden, born December 22, 2007. Hayden is five years old this year. He is well-loved and spoiled by his parents and by Phillip and Louise.

Phillip has been a great father-in-law. He was already a great friend. He was already like my second dad. I am glad he is the grandfather to my son.

Eric Walden,
Heather Lim Walden
baby Hayden

Heidi Lim

Louise Lim

Chapter Twenty-three

The Night of the Long Gun

In the Chinese culture the number 8 is believed to carry the meaning of infinity. It is also used as a sign of good luck. If you buy a car tag in Malaysia, it might cost $100, buy the same tag having any one of its numerals to be 8 and you will gladly pay $100,000. There is a long waiting list for such tags. Also, houses or apartments that cost $100,000 will easily sell for three or maybe even four times that much if the address includes an 8 in the location. The list of individuals wanting to own property with an 8 in the location goes on into infinity. Couples who plan to have children count back 8 months from August and try for the pregnancy during the month of December. Such as it goes with the number 8.

The event I am about to describe to you occurred on August 8, 2007. That is the 8th month, on the 8th day. Did this date bring luck to my family? You can judge. Luck that we lived through it for sure.

Do you feel safe in your home at night? Do you trust the American legal system? My perspective about life and willingness to trust the American legal system changed abruptly one night.

My thoughts-the feeling of being safe and secure in my own home-changed forever for me as quickly as you can snap your fingers on August 8, 2007. This is date when I almost died during home invasion. It was bad, bad time in my life. The night of the long gun.

Before I tell you about this event, I would like to ask question. If thug pointed loaded gun at you and said he was going to kill you, would you beg for your life? It is a situation I hope you never have to face. Do you know what you would do when faced with choice of life or death?

Have you ever been put to this test?

Now that I know what I would do, I think back to my great-grandfather Lim Keng who traveled towards freedom for 60 days aboard sampan with 16 other men. What did he do to survive? If given choice, would he eat human flesh in order to survive? What would you do? We think we would never do this thing that is so aberrant, but when truly faced with ravaging hunger and possibility of dying on small sampan instead of traveling on to freedom, what would you do?

We often say, "I'm hungry." But, none of us actually know what true hunger feels like.

What would real hunger drive you do to? I think Lim Keng had inner strength to do what he had to do to survive because, out of 16, he was one of 6 who did survive.

Would you eat human flesh to live? Would you beg for your life when confronted with life or death situation?

I found out that I possess same qualities of great Lim Keng. I know that his strength and ability to survive live in my DNA.

On August 8, 2007, I learned that I, Phillip Lim, great-grandson of esteemed Lim Keng would beg for his life when thug pointed gun at him and said, "I will kill you. I will kill you."

Thug said these words to me when I tried to call 9-1-1 with my cell phone.

"Please don't kill me," I begged. "I have beautiful children.

Listen to my story and decide, what would you do?

August 8, 2007 began as non-eventful night for my family. At approximately midnight, I was at home with two of my children, Shawn, then age 19, and Heidi who was 13 that year. My wife, Louise, was at work at hospital where she is registered nurse. All of sudden, I heard noise and in blink of an eye, four masked men were inside my kitchen.

I had been watching television and drinking soup upstairs in our house when in an instant, life changed, three or maybe four thugs wearing bandanas over their faces came into room where I was standing. One of thugs was black man who flashed gun in my face and said, "I will kill you. I will kill you."

The thought flashed through my mind, "Is this real? Is this night I am going to die?"

Why do I call four men who entered my house thugs? No one wearing a bandana over face is nice person. Up to no good. Thieves. Murderers. Thugs.

I heard sounds of someone screaming and realized sounds were coming from me. Thugs were yelling back and me. One white man hit me on back with baseball bat. He wanted to know if I had drugs. "No, I don't have any drugs," I screamed at him. I was running around in house trying to avoid strikes from the ball bat.

"Call 9-1-1; Call 9-1-1, Help!" I screamed.

I picked up barstool and threw it at man with gun. I ran downstairs to second living room and children's bedrooms. Bandana-man followed me down steps, hitting me with bat again and again. I hit back using my fists, but he continued to beat me with bat. I ran into my daughter's room to make sure she was safe, but she was not in her room. I was able to hold door to her room shut for few minutes, but thug shoved his way inside room and hit me more times. I ran into downstairs living room. I'm still screaming.

Bandana-man followed me and hit with bat more and more. I fought him off with the only weapons I had, my arms. At one point, I fell onto couch and man demanded, "Give me your jewelry and your wallet."

I pulled wallet from pocket and began removing gold bracelet he wanted. I could not grip bracelet enough to get it off my wrist. I had injured my thumb at work and it was still swollen. I handed him wallet.

Bandana-man all the cash in it which was $60-three twenties. Thug also yanked gold bracelet off my arm and pulled telephone cord out of wall. I am thinking, thug going to kill me for three twenties and a gold bracelet?

At that point, I fumbled and was able to get cell phone out of pocket and quickly tried to dial 9-1-1. Thief grabbed phone out of my hand and broke into two pieces. My actions made invader even angrier. He hit me more viciously with baseball bat.

I screamed and ran away from him, trying to hit back. Suddenly, second invader began beating me with bat, too.

I continued to scream. "Call 9-l-l; call 9-l-l. Help." My only protection was to cross my arms in front of face to keep bat from hitting my eyes or knocking my teeth out.

When the invasion began, my son, Shawn and daughter, Heidi, were downstairs. Heidi heard me say, "Call 9-l-1; "call 9-1-1; Help." She immediately grabbed cordless phone, dialed 9-1-1 and ran into her brother's room to find Shawn. When she could not find Shawn, she hid herself under bed. She remained on phone with

9-1-1 operator providing details and instructions about how sheriff's deputies could get to our house.

It was Heidi's quick thinking and her willingness to obey her father's screams that saved us. Heidi was our guardian angel. Heidi was screaming into phone, but thugs did not hear her. They didn't even know she was in house. I believe Holy Spirit blocked screams from Heidi so that thugs did not hear them.

When I yelled, "Call 9-1-1. Help," my son Shawn ran upstairs to see what was going on. Shawn was met by tall, black male with bandana over his face holding big gun. Shawn grabbed barrel of gun on side and struggled with the man. He could not see me, but he heard commotion in kitchen. Suddenly, someone hit Shawn on back of his head with baseball bat. Shawn blacked out. He fell over couch and was beaten severely by one white man with bat and by black man using butt of gun.

When Shawn regained consciousness, man with bat left room, but man with gun told him to go into bathroom. Shawn's head was bleeding profusely. He asked man if he could reach for towel and man said that he could. Shawn grabbed towel and placed on his head.

Blood spurted out of his head like a water faucet had been turned on. Floors in both rooms were covered with Shawn's bright, red blood.

While he was in bathroom, he could hear someone walking through house and he could see shadowy figure walking up and down hallway. He could also hear my screams and assumed that I was fighting attacker and was being hurt.

Shawn kept his wits about him and was able to count. One thug holding Shawn in bathroom. One thug, maybe two fighting with me. One thug walking up and down hallway. Three, for sure; maybe four thugs.

We discovered later that shadowy figure found briefcase located in my bedroom closet because it had been opened. It was full of expensive jewelry, but none was missing.

Again, I believe our guardian angel made the jewelry invisible to thugs. Thugs didn't take jewelry because they didn't see it.

While I was being beaten, I knew, if this thug pulls the trigger, I will be dead. All I could see was big loaded gun pointed to my face. Do you know how big a gun looks when it is pointed at you?

Heidi stayed on phone for about seven to eight minutes with 9-1-1 operator until police arrived. Heidi kept cool head; saved Shawn; saved me.

When thugs saw officers entering house, they gave up and stopped beating Shawn and me. One invader jumped out of window and has never been identified. One hid in closet in my bedroom and was found when deputies searched house. Two who were beating on Shawn and me were immediately placed in handcuffs. Police handcuffed us, too. Weird.

It was not until thugs were arrested and transported to jail that we realized how badly we were hurt. Paramedics loaded us onto gurneys, put us in ambulances and drove us to University of Tennessee Hospital.

The trauma team determined that my thumb was broken. I could not raise my hand above my shoulder and my head was split open. I had black and blue marks from the top of head to the tips of feet. I was hit by the bats as many as twenty-five to thirty times. Huge red blotches appeared on my skin. I was in extreme pain in back, legs and arms for months after attack. Was sent for physical therapy and counseling.

Shawn had cuts and bruises all over his body. Large cut on his head that required fifteen staples in his head in order to close wound. He was in extreme pain and was given medication that he said barely cut the pain. He stayed in bed for over a week and was stiff and sore for many weeks after attack.

Damages to house could only be described as saying house looked like it had been hit by tornado. Crooks ruined good couch and mattress, broke doors and windows, and demolished cell phone.

Worse part was blood everywhere. Have you ever seen house with blood on walls and floors? Man, it is horrible.

Wound on Shawn's head had caused him to lose lot of blood. Trail of red blood on carpet ran from steps to downstairs living room into bathroom. Blood splatter was on furniture and walls of several rooms. Our house looked like the place where they filmed that movie "The Texas Chainsaw Murders"; a frightening sight.

Total damages to our house were estimated to be $20,000.

Thugs had no shame. They even hurt dog. After things settled down that night, Heidi remembered that our dog, Chubb, was outside in fenced yard. She searched for Chubb and found him cowering under furniture in back yard; Chubb hiding from thugs.

It broke my heart for Louise, my wife, to see damage thugs did to our beautiful house. She works so hard to keep everything spotless.

Since I was in hospital, I could not be there with her when she went back to house. I could not protect her from this sight.

She reportedly was overwhelmed with emotions and cried her heart out. Who would not cry to see these things? She said she kept wondering how we survived with all blood that was in that house. Louise is nurse. She knows about blood.

Shawn's testimony:
In April of 2010, when the case finally made it to trial, Shawn testified that on the night of August 8, 2007, he was downstairs and getting ready for bed. Suddenly, he heard his father upstairs yelling, "Call 9-1-1, help." Shawn said he was scared and did not know what was going on. He ran upstairs and saw a tall, black male with a bandana over his face holding a gun. Shawn grabbed the gun and struggled with the man. He said he could see his father but heard "other commotion" in the kitchen area.

Suddenly, someone hit him on the back of his head with a baseball bat. He said he blacked out for a moment, fell over the couch, and was beaten with the bat and the butt of the gun. He said two men told him, "Don't try and be brave or anything, sit down, stay right here."

While the men were with him, Shawn said he could hear his father screaming downstairs. The man with the bat left, and the man with the gun moved Shawn to a bathroom. Shawn grabbed a towel and held it to his head. The man with the gun told Shawn to sit in the bathroom and the man stayed with him until the police arrived. Shawn said that while he was in the bathroom he could see someone with a baseball bat walking 'back and forth," searching the upstairs bedrooms. He said he could still hear his father and a commotion downstairs.

Shawn testified that he heard the man with the bat alert the man with the gun that the two men tried to find a way out of the house, and that he heard a bedroom window break.

Shawn saw a police officer, and Phillip Lim came upstairs. The police began searching the house and found the man with the bat and the man with the gun hiding in an upstairs bedroom. The police brought them out of the room and took off their bandanas. Shawn said that only one of the intruders was black, and he identified Mills in court as the black intruder with the gun. Regarding an in-court identification of Spencer, Shawn said that "it was dark in the living room, so I'm not sure if he was the one that was in the living room or the one downstairs that I didn't see."

Shawn said that as a result of the attack, he had a large cut on his head that had to be closed with fifteen staples. He also had cuts and bruises on his body. He said he was in extreme pain, took pain medication, and stayed in bed for about one week. He said that the home invasion lasted about ten minutes and that he was "out of it" when he talked with the police.

Shawn said that he saw two men during the attack and "heard others." Shawn said that while the man with the bat and the man with the gun were upstairs with him, he could hear his father downstairs yelling "...like he was still getting beaten."

Heidi's testimony:
Heidi Lim testified that on the night of August 8, 2007, she was downstairs in her bedroom, which was next to Shawn's bedroom, and heard her father upstairs yelling "help, call 9-1-1." She grabbed a cordless telephone and went into Shawn's bedroom, but Shawn was not there. Heidi heard yelling upstairs, but she did not hear Shawn. She dialed 9-1-1 and got down on the floor, trying to hide.

The State played Heidi's 9-1-1 call for the jury. During the call, which lasted about seven minutes, Heidi told the operator that someone was in her house and that she was hiding in her brother's bedroom. She also told the operator that she could hear someone saying, "get on the ground" and that she thought her father had been hurt.

Heidi testified that when the police arrived, she ran upstairs. Her father and brother were in the bathroom, and she saw Shawn holding a towel to his bleeding head. She said that her family owned a mixed-breed dog that stayed outside in a fenced yard, that she later found the dog hiding in a basement bathroom, and that his eye was bleeding.

Reaction to Home Invasion From Louise Lim:
On the night my husband and step-son were so savagely beaten, everything at our house had been typical. I remember doing laundry, talking to the children and my husband, hugging and kissing him good-bye, and driving to work. Then, about two hours into my shift at the hospital where I am an orthopedic nurse, I got a call from one of my dearest friends who told me to try and remain calm because he had some bad news. He told me that Phillip and Shawn were alive, but both had been hurt during a home invasion. No one knew for sure exactly what had happened, but he was on his way to get me and drive me to the hospital where they had taken Phillip and Shawn. By then, he was only able to tell me a few sketchy details saying that both Phillip and Shawn had been beaten with a baseball bat and Shawn had a huge gash in his skull and had lost a lot of blood.

Upon hearing this news, my knees nearly buckled, I began breathing heavily and was almost thrown into a full panic attack. I called upon my training as a nurse to pull me through this ordeal.

Once we arrived at the hospital, I was taken straight to Phillip who was still in the ER. As we hurried through the hospital corridor, the doctor who greeted me said that Shawn was in surgery for head injuries and that he had lost a lot of blood.

When I approached Phillip's bed, I could not believe that this person they were showing me was my husband Phillip. His eyes were swollen shut, his face was a blurred mass of red and purple pounded flesh. His arms were black and blue and he was moaning in pain.

Tears that I could not stop popped out of my eyes and I felt their hotness.

I squeezed Phillip's hand and whispered into his ear, "Phillip, it's Louise. I am here. I love you." I kissed him even though my tears were falling so quickly I could not wipe them away fast enough. Phillip squeezed my hand and groaned.

"Shawn?" he asked through swollen lips. Tears were running down his face, too. "They are doing everything they can for him," I replied.

For the rest of that night and most of the next day, I stayed right there beside him and all we could both do was bawl. We had searched a lifetime and were a world apart when we finally found each other. I could not bear to lose him in such a violent and senseless way.

I checked on Shawn; sat with Phillip. Checked on Shawn; sat with Phillip. This is how I spent my time. I was also shaking, crying, praying and remained fearful all night.

Chapter Twenty-four

Recovery and justice

It took several months before Shawn and I began to feel like our old selves again. We endured pain in our bodies and emotional upheaval to our spirits. The feeling of safety and security we had always had when we closed the doors of our house to the outside world were destroyed. Never again will we be content with the normal sounds made in everyday living. All it takes is the slam of car door closing, or sudden knock or bump in the night to transport our minds back to that awful night.

The damages to our house were repaired, but how do you ever repair damages to your mind? Believe me, you don't.

Justice crept by like a snail crawling on gritty sand for the four thugs who invaded our home. It was April 2010, over two years, before their cases even came in front of judge. Kept us upset all the time; back and forth with lawyers. Back and forth. Make you dizzy to keep up with it all.

One thug smashed window and ran from the house and no one would ever tell who he was. One pled guilty and was sentenced to seven years in jail. Two were charged with two counts of especially aggravated kidnapping, one county of especially aggravated robbery, both Class A felonies, and one count of aggravated burglary, a Class C felony. Those two were found guilty and sentenced to 25 years for the Class A felonies and another 6 years in prison for the Class C felony. However, in the revolving door of our justice system, one thug appealed his conviction and won. He walked free after nearly killing Shawn and me.

Do you understand that justice is blind? I do

Healing of the body takes time. Healing of the spirit and emotions takes even longer. We pulled together as a family. We also went to counseling. I continue to have times when I am startled awake from deep sleep with thoughts of thugs beating me. So does Shawn.

Our Mission statement

Phillip Lim tries out his new seats.

Chapter Twenty-five

Asia Café is born

So much of my life I could record in these pages. However, there is not enough time to go into details of everything. Do you see now, the rollercoaster ride?

The rollercoaster went up to the top in 2006 with my marriage to Louise, but down again in 2007 with the home invasion. By 2009, it was on the way back up to the top. My dream of owning my own restaurant was coming true. Asia Cafe is born.

At one point, I had owned restaurants in Malaysia. This gave me experience in the restaurant business. I wanted to open my own place in Knoxville. Asia Café came from this dream. At last I saw my ideas and plans become reality.

Searching for right spot for new business is exhausting. My brother, Jimmy, my wife, Louise, and I spent hours, days even, looking and thinking-this place or that? What are attributes of one location as opposed to another? What can we afford? Finally, it was settled, we chose 6714 B North Central Avenue in Knoxville, Tennessee. There were several reasons for this selection, but, as they say about real estate, it is location, location, location. Also, in Malaysia, the number 6 means wealth. The number 8 means infinity. Malaysians pay big dollars to have these numbers in their addresses or on their car tags.

The underlying theme we chose for Asia Café is "Where East Meets West." This describes my life as well, right? We knew that if we would prepare traditional Asian recipes as our mother, grandmother and other relatives have cooked in Malaysia, that the customers who know the authentic tastes would find us. They did.

What makes Asia Café popular? We are the only place far and wide where you can find six kinds of Asian food-Thai, Japanese Grill, Malaysian, Oriental, Indonesian, and Sushi.

We're a fun place, too. We include entertainment. Karaoke is big, really big. We have regulars who come each week to sing. We do country music and Rock and Roll. What the people want. This is what we do. We have LED lighted tables for enjoyment. People soak in atmosphere with flickering lights sparkling in their faces. We serve cold beer and provide Carry Out and Delivery.

Each year we have Bikini Contest and Halloween Costume Contest. These are fun and draw big crowds; standing room only. We have Biker Night-reminds me of Chinese gangs from my youth. Host big Christmas party for staff and friends, too.

We have already been voted Best Ethnic Restaurant in this area. We have been on television several times. Plenty of articles have been written about us in local newspapers. We are topic of blogs. We have plenty loyal customers.

I myself work from 60 to 80 hours a week to make this success. Customers love me. They like my personality. I am a people person.

Asia Café has 27 full time employees. My cooks have experience. They understand the specific ways to prepare the traditional foods. Asian food must be cooked and served hot-hot temperatures as well as hot seasonings. We also use the correct kinds of pots for cooking. Ones that can endure the high temperatures.

Everything is done the right way, using the old ways.

Before I hire a cook, I ask him to go to kitchen and prepare a recipe on our menu. I am looking for a certain taste, without it, I will not hire you. Some cooks just love salt; some use no salt. Our recipes must be consistent. I expect excellence from all employees, and I get it. We have a great team.

Our customers tell me they drive from long distances to get the taste of the real ethic and exotic foods. Do you eat chicken feet? We serve them. Good. Some people really like them, some say, "I never eat this."

What we are doing is working. We have success with our business plan. Recession proof. Economy did not effect us. We did well, even better. Our customers keep it that way. I know how to do something for the USA economy-create jobs. I am a job creator. USA needs to ask me and other businessmen how to do this. The answer. Find a need and fill it. People have got to eat. Feed them well; keep prices acceptable and they will reward you by returning for more.

Chapter Twenty-six

My future is bright

What is next? We are ready to expand. The time is right. Our second store, Asia Café West, is opening in March 2013. We are fierce and seizing an opportunity in an area of town known for wealth. While others are closing their businesses, we are opening a new one because we will have less competition.

Once again it took much searching, but we found a great location near a very busy intersection. Address has 8 in it. It is right time. We are ready to move forward.

Do I get tired? Yes. Exhausted? Yes. However, my life is easy compared to what my great-grandfather faced.

As I go about my busy day, my heart pumps blood through my body. This blood contains the strength handed down through the years to me by my ancestor. He faced the ocean, the hot sun beating down on him for sixty days. The fear. The departure from the first wife he loved so much. The back breaking work tapping latex in temperatures that soared to over 100 degrees. I tell myself, if he can do all that, I can face fatigue. I can face computer systems crashing and fitful children and relatives who want to borrow money.

What am I saying? My problems, whatever they may be, are small. Lim Keng is the man who made the real sacrifices. He did it for me, for all of his descendents.

As I look back over my life, there is long list of people who have influenced me and helped me to be successful. The most was, of course, my great-grandfather Lim Keng. Without his escape from China nothing would be possible for my family. He is the person who made all of our lives better. He brought us into freedom. Without freedom dreams cannot be reached.

Next, would be my grandfather who also shared his wealth with me and gave excellent counsel. Also, grandmothers and grandfather from other side of family helped me out a lot.

My father and mother are also in this list. They provided wonderful upbringing for me. My father made certain his children had best of everything. He worked long hours and was good father and great businessman; fine example to us. My mother was one I turned to with my problems. I always wound up at her door when I had exhausted all other means of financial support. I often cried crocodile tears to her. She always came through. She gave me money. She spoke softly to me in times of trouble. My godfather, Honorable RR Chelvarajah, belongs on this list as do far too many others to continue listing.

My future is now with Louise. She has been very good wife. She is responsible. Works hard and is an excellent example. Keeps house spotless. We have fun together hanging out. We laugh a lot. She fun person. Understands me very well. Her family has also been a great source of love and comfort.

Shawn is doing well by following me into restaurant business. Barry is still a part of me. I hope we can experience more closeness in the future. My girls, Heather and Heidi, have grown into productive, responsible, educated women. Heather and Eric have given me one grandson. I hope for others from my other children when time right.

I love my children and everyone in my family and think being a father and member of Lim family have been my best projects.

Time was right for new restaurant. Time right also to record my story-the story of how Phillip Lim continues the family dynasty by recording the story of how Lim Keng escaped to riches.   THE END

Great-grandfather Lim Keng

Hayden Walden, Phillip and Louise's grandson

Heidi Lim, Jimmy Lim, Hayden Walden, Louise Lim, Eric Walden, Phillip Lim, Heather Lim Walden, and Shawn Lim

Front Row: George' wife Doreen Siah Kim Neo, George's mother Liau Ah Moi, George Lim Cheng Hock.

Back Row: George's son-in-law Tan Kok Tiong, Georges's daughter Cynthia Lim Swee Chen, George's youngest son Benjamin Lim Boon Zhong and George's oldest son Randy Lim Boon Heng.

APPENDIX

Published in Infinity International Power, Inc. Newsletter in 2007.
Mr. Phillip Lim, one of the founding members of the Infinity International Power, Inc., is the Chairman of the company.

He is widely known in the Far East and is very well respected by his close allies. One of the key elements to his success is partly due to his sincere commitment in the involvement of the manufacturing sector and the great support from family members.

Voted BEST Chinese Restaurant in Knoxville: 2010 by City Voter from WTNZFOX 43-Hot List

The results are In! Congratulations to Asia Cafe, named #1 Chinese Restaurant in Knoxville on the 2010 wtnzfox43.com Hot List. Chosen out of 7,563 total votes; 4,839 total voters.

Asia Café - A Popular Dining Spot March 31, 2011
By Martha Rose Woodward

If you are looking for tasty food from an authentic Asian cuisine, type 6714 B Central Avenue Pike, 37912 into your GPS and head on out to the Asia Cafe off I-75-Exit 110 Callahan Drive.

Owners Louise and Phillip Lim, along with family members and their highly skilled and well-trained staff, will greet you with a smile and dazzle you with a choice of six kinds of ethnic Asian foods—all under one roof. Choose from the "all Asian, healthy, exotic recipes" of Malaysian, Thai, Oriental, Indonesian, Sushi or Japanese Grill.

Lim, a gregarious, lively, mannerly gentleman, is a native of Malaysia, who says he has lived in Knoxville since 1995 and has been in the restaurant business in one position or he other for over 28 years. He has lived in the USA for 30 years; his wife, whom he describes as beautiful and smart, has been an RN for 20 years and currently works at St. Mary's Hospital located in North Knoxville.

His son, Shawn, has also worked in the restaurant. Asia Cafe was voted Knoxville's #1 Best Ethnic and Chinese Restaurant of the Year.

The Lim family is also the owner of Natural Alternatives, Inc., a company that sells supplements that "give you natural healthy alternatives that matter."

Another company owned by his family is a distributor of gasoline and oil and is a leader in advanced separation technology with over 30 years of experience combined. It can be found at www. Infinityintlpower.com

According to their web site: asiacafe.org "Lim has received numerous merit and achievement awards and has recognition throughout his career.

He is a businessman with extensive knowledge and experience in the food and beverage industry, as well as in the import and export industry. Through his many years of experience and entrepreneurial skills, he has been responsible for the success of numerous business ventures.

Lim is a master in the food and beverage service industry. He worked for many years ground up from a dishwasher to management position in a famous family dining restaurant chain in the US. He then exercised his experience and started a small to-go and catering restaurant. Having built it from scratch, he expanded his ideas and successfully conceived a chain of catering and franchising restaurants here and abroad.

In 1995, he was named restaurant entrepreneur in the Melaka Tourism Industry Magazine in Malaysia, with worldwide distribution." Lim says that his restaurant has been recession proof as people who know what it means to find good food truly prepared the Asian way have flocked to his store. Lim has expanded his business once and is looking at opening three more restaurants possibly in Hardin Valley, Maryville and Oak Ridge.

Lim attributes the success of his business to his use of the "Secret recipes he brought over from Malaysia as well as authentic cooking methods."

"Asian food is meant to be served hot," he said. "When cooked correctly, the aromas spill out from the kitchen to the delight of our customers." Asia Café also takes the extra steps to provide free Wi-Fi for customers who enjoy working while dining, and they have live entertainment every Friday, Saturday, and Sunday nights.

Elvis Tribute Artist, Ronnie Miller, is a regular performer along with a live band on Saturdays, Karaoke every Friday and Bike Night Sundays. The creative businessman is the in process of developing an energy drink he plans to market soon that he says will provide vitality in all aspects of a person's life.

With a grand flair for theatrics, Lim recently installed two commodes as seating in place of chairs in one dining room of his restaurant. Ever the showman, Lim says, "Come to Asia Café--first restaurant in America to have toilet seats as chairs."

Phillip Lim, owner of Asia Cafe in Knoxville, TN, says his restaurant is the first in the nation to replace two diners' chairs with commodes. "You can sit on the throne in my restaurant," says Lim.

Phillip Lim Speaks at Northside Kiwanis Club March 30, 2012
by Martha Rose Woodward

Phillip Lim, owner of Asia Café, located at 6714 Central Avenue Pike # B Knoxville, TN 37912, (865) 688-8888, was the guest speaker on Wednesday, March 21 for the meeting of the Northside Kiwanis Club at the Foundry in World's Fair Park.

Lim, an immigrant of Chinese descent, born in Malaysia spoke about the history of his family. Lim said he could not speak about his own successes as a businessman without beginning with the decision made by his great-grandfather to stow away on a ship leaving China in order to escape the brutality of the government. Lim said his ancestor landed in Malaysia with empty pockets being only one out of many to survive the arduous trip.

Lim explained how his great-grandfather took a job as a cutter in the rubber fields and went on to own a rubber factory.

Lim said that because of his great-grandfather, he always had everything he ever wanted. Describing himself as "a brat", Lim explained how his father and grandfather sent him to America in order to teach him the value of money.

Lim said that he had watched a lot of American television programs as a child and teenager and loved the Westerns—Gunsmoke, Wagon Train, Have Gun; Will Travel, John Wayne, Clint Eastwood— so he was happy to travel to America searching for cowboys and Indians.

Lim said he arrived in California with $300 in Traveler's Checks in his pocket and expected to get off the plane and see horses, wagons and cowboys, but he did not see them.

Lim kept the audience entertained with his journey as he also traveled to Houston, Texas, where he finally did see some cowboys, but they were not riding horses, but were driving pick-up trucks.

The group enjoyed Lim's speech so much they have asked him to come back soon and continue with more details about his amazing life.

According to the web site for Asia Café, " Mr. Lim received his early education in Melaka, Malaysia. He attended Preston College of TAFE in Melbourne, Australia with studies in sales and advertising. He further attended courses in success and leadership at Dale Carnegie in Birmingham. Following these achievements, he then was successfully accepted at University of Phoenix for his studies in Bachelor of Science degree in Business Marketing.

He has received numerous merit and achievement awards and has recognition throughout his career. He is a businessman with extensive knowledge and experience in the food and beverage industry, as well as in the import and export industry. Through his many years of experience and entrepreneurial skills, he has been responsible for the success of numerous business ventures.

In year 1995, he was named restaurant entrepreneur in the Melaka Tourism Industry Magazine in Malaysia."

Asia Café has been voted #1 Best Ethic and Chinese Restaurant in Knoxville on several occasions.

Lim is grateful for the accolades and said that the ingredients to success begin with hard work and the great support from loyal family members.

Phillip Lim

Phillip's Invention: Bio-Vital Health drink

Bio-Vital-The Future of Vitality Heighten your sexual vitality, energy level and stamina. Bio-Vital is the proprietary blend of herbal complexes that can truly make a difference in your life.

Being larger is not impossible and it doesn't require surgery, prescriptions, gadgets or exercises.

Sexual Vitality

Sexual energy and the body's overall vitality not only determines the quality of sex that both men and women enjoy with their partners, it plays a large role in the overall happiness and the sense of well being felt throughout the other areas of life. Bio-Vital strives to increase vitality and happiness with its patent pending formula in every aspect of life in a way never before seen until now.

These formula are designed for:

• Better Sex • Increased Sensations • Strength • Happiness • Endurance • Vitality • More Intense Orgasms • Size • Energy • Burn Fat • Immune system. It has been approved by the FDA for human consumption.

Content copyright 2011-2012. BIOVITALDRINK.COM. All rights reserved.

Mr. Phillip Lim, one of the founding members of Bio-Vital, Inc., is the Chairman of the company and the inventor.

Born in Malaysia, Lim received his early education in Melaka, Malaysia. He attended Preston College of TAFE in Melbourne, Australia with studies

Phillip Lim and Walt Wojnar at the Kiwanis Club 2011.

in sales and advertising. He further attended courses in success and leadership at Dale Carnegie in Birmingham, Alabama.

Following these achievements, he then was successfully accepted at University of Phoenix, Phoenix Arizona for his Bachelor of Science degree in Business Marketing.

He has received numerous achievement awards and recognition throughout his career. He is a businessman with extensive knowledge and experience in the food and beverage industry, as well as the import and export industry. Through his many years of experience and entrepreneurial skills, he has been responsible for the success of numerous business ventures and inventions.

These include revisionary developments in the areas of eco-friendly Oil and Gas distributions to successful passing of the torch onto the third generation of family businessmen to make advancement in health for the international nutrition industry.

The last 28 years and inherited knowledge from his family have made Lim a master in the food, beverage, and nutritional industry. He worked for many years from a dishwasher to a management position in a famous family dining restaurant chain in the US. He then exercised his experience and started a small to-go and catering restaurant.

Having built it from scratch, he expanded his ideas and successfully conceived a chain of catering and franchising restaurants in Malaysia. In 1995, he was named restaurant entrepreneur in the Melaka Tourism Industry magazine in Malaysia with worldwide distribution.

With his diverse background and experience as well as many international business contacts, Phillip Lim will be a valuable asset to the growth and success of BioVital, Inc.

He is widely known in the Far East and is very well respected by his close allies. One of the key elements to his success is partly due to his sincere commitment in the involvement of the manufacturing sector and the great support from family members.

Bibliography:

http://asiacafe.org/about us/news
http://asianhistory.about.com/od/malaysia/p/malaysiaprof.htm
Asian Pacific Post Magazine, 6, 2006
http://www.chenghoonteng.org.my/p1authenticity.html
http://www.geographia.com/malaysia/history05.htm
http://www. Infinityintlpower.com
Infinity International Power, Inc. Newsletter in 2007.
http://www.theknoxvillejournal.com
http://www.knoxvillenewssentinel.com
Lim, David, family history
Lim, Gary, photographs of Melaka, Malaysia, 2013
Malaysian Bar Council, Leboh Pasar Besar, 50050 Kuala Lumpur, Malaysia
http://www.pshcebu.com/
http://www.sears.com-wooden pillow
http://www.streetdirectory.com.my/travel_guide/malaysia/malaysia_fast_facts/93/title_in
_malaysia.php
http://www.tourism.gov.my/en/us
http://www.umsl.edu/services/govdocs/wofact97/153.htm
http://en.wikipedia.org/wiki/Malaysia
http://en.wikipedia.org/wiki/Pillow

Elvis Tribute Artist, Ronnie Miller, is a regular performer at the Asia Cafe.

Asia Cafe West opened at 8111 Gleason Road, Knoxville, Tennessee in March 2013

Phillip's own Shrimp Sauce.

Other Books by Martha Rose Woodward

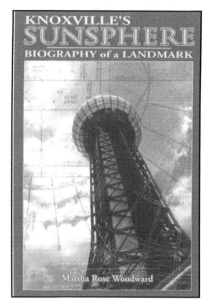

Knoxville's Sunsphere

Biography of a Landmark , a 208 page, nonfiction book, was published in September 2007 by Video Publishing and Printing, Schad Road, in Knoxville, Tennessee, Tim Carroll, publisher. The author is Martha Rose Woodward, a retired school teacher, who turned her creative talents into a part-time career by going to work for a local newspaper, The Knoxville Journal.

Woodward's book uses personification to turn the unique tower which was built as the theme structure for the 1982 World's Fair, into a person. "The Sunpshere has had an interesting life during the last 26 years and I thought it was a story that needed to be told," said Woodward. With input from the architect who dreamed up the building, William Denton, former Mayor Randy Tyree, and Jesse Barr, financial advisor to the Sunsphere, Woodward conducted most of the research for her book at the East Tennessee History Center as well as through personal interviews. "If anyone has walked in and out of the Sunsphere during the last twenty-five years, Martha has interviewed them," said William Denton of Woodward's attention to detail.

The book is available for sale at www. Amazon. Com and from the author at Sunsphere book @ aol.com.

Knoxville's 1982 World's Fair

Debuted on February 16, 2009 to brisk sales. From May 1 through October 31, 1982, Knoxville hosted the world's fair based on the theme "Energy Turns the World." Expo '82 was the first world's fair to be held in the southeastern United States in 97 years, hosting 22 countries and more than 11 million people. Once referred to as the "scruffy little city by the Tennessee River," Knoxville provided one big party for people to visit from all over to witness the live entertainment, parades, displays, exhibits, musical and sporting events, food, costumes, rides, games, and arcades. The news reports of the day declared the "World Came to Knoxville" as it hosted the official international exposition, fully licensed and sanctioned by the Bureau des Expositions Internationales in Paris, France. This book was published by Arcadia Publishing from Mt. Pleasant, South Carolina.

Made in the USA
San Bernardino, CA
03 May 2015